"Read it and weep—joyfully! This [ ] carefully interweaves biblical exege[ ] mation and rejection from the diver[ ] [ ] of humble sisters in Christ. We are reminded that time is short, our mandate is clear, and King Jesus is glorious—yet we are weak and fearful, preoccupied, and inward looking. I love the book's insistence on prayerful dependence on God to work, and the soul-burning witness to his answers to these prayers. We are repeatedly encouraged to know our Savior better, that we may proclaim the riches of his grace more fully and with greater nuance and sensitivity to context. It's a book I want every Christian woman I know to read—because nothing matters more!"

Fiona Millar, Lecturer, Queensland Theological College

"Each and every day the Lord sends his people out all over the world with the same glorious commission: 'Go and make disciples.' *Joyfully Spreading the Word* shares faithful examples of disciple making in places of employment, universities, neighborhoods, and homes—rightly reminding us that wherever we are, we have the privilege of sharing the Word with others. This book will encourage and inspire you to see the mission field in your own backyard."

Melissa Kruger, Editor, The Gospel Coalition; author, *Walking with God in the Season of Motherhood* and *In All Things*

"Have you been longing to share the gospel with your friends and neighbors but have been hesitant to initiate? If so, *Joyfully Spreading the Word* is the perfect place to begin. We all know that we should evangelize, yet most of us feel guilty that we rarely do it. This winsome collection from various writers reminded me of the daily opportunities I have to share my faith and gives me courage and tools to follow through. These women offer practical examples from everyday life, which makes this book so helpful. Read it—you'll be stirred afresh to share the best news in the world!"

Vaneetha Rendall Risner, author, *The Scars That Have Shaped Me*

"This great book was written by women, but its content is for everyone. The authors truly understand what the Great Commission is all about. It is about not only proclaiming the gospel message, but about living it out every day and in every place. 'The ambassador for Christ is never off duty,' to use one of the many gospel phrases found in this book. By this, the authors mean that, regardless of where you live, work, or even visit, as a redeemed person, you are expected to live and share the good news of our Redeemer. Jesus said to go and make disciples, but if we are to live the gospel in everyday life, then we never stop going. That is the challenge in this book. Please buy, read, and apply this book. It is worthy."

Miguel Núñez, Senior Pastor, International Baptist Church, Santo Domingo, Dominican Republic; President and Founder, Wisdom and Integrity Ministries

"*Joyfully Spreading the Word* is refreshingly rooted in delight rather than duty. It is a clarion call compelling all women to go, make disciples, and teach his commandments, coupled with the gentle reminder of the great comfort that he is with us always, to the end of the age."

Karen Hodge, Women's Ministry Coordinator, The Presbyterian Church in America; author, *Transformed: Life-taker to Life-giver*

"Biblical teaching, combined with personal examples and stories, make this book a warmhearted challenge for women to engage their everyday worlds with the gospel of Jesus Christ. Be encouraged by it, then take a risk and share your faith with someone around you."

Mack and Leeann Stiles, authors, *Mack & Leeann's Guide to Short-Term Missions and Evangelism: How the Whole Church Speaks of Jesus*

"At heart, I'm a hesitant evangelist—and I don't like that. 'What should I say? How should I say it? Who would listen?' That's why I can heartily recommend *Joyfully Spreading the Word*. This theologically sound, guilt-free book answers those questions. Through a collection of stories and a variety of role models, it inspires readers with both the privilege and the urgency of the biblical mandate to go and share 'the sacred writings, which are able to make you wise for salvation through faith in Christ Jesus' (2 Tim. 3:15). Read it, use it, and see if God won't indeed prove through your life that his Word will not return empty, but will accomplish that which he purposes (Isa. 55:11)."

Jani Ortlund, Executive Vice President, Renewal Ministries

"A desire to reach the lost has often been the gate through which all sorts of unhelpful things have gained entrance into the church. And so I am grateful that *Joyfully Spreading the Word* is what so many books on evangelism are not: engaging and humane while still clear and faithful. I found each chapter to be thought provoking, challenging, and full of insight. As I read it, I found myself both scheming about ways to share the gospel in my circles, and also making a list of other people I wanted to point toward this resource. I recommend it wholeheartedly."

Mike McKinley, Pastor, Sterling Park Baptist Church; author, *Church in Hard Places*; *Am I Really a Christian?*; and *Church Planting Is for Wimps*

Joyfully Spreading
the Word

Other Crossway titles by The Gospel Coalition

Don't Call It a Comeback: The Old Faith for a New Day, edited by Kevin DeYoung (2011)

God's Love Compels Us: Taking the Gospel to the World, edited by D. A. Carson and Kathleen B. Nielson (2015)

The Gospel as Center: Renewing Our Faith and Reforming Our Ministry Practices, edited by D. A. Carson and Timothy Keller (2012)

Here Is Our God: God's Revelation of Himself in Scripture, edited by Kathleen B. Nielson and D. A. Carson (2014)

His Mission: Jesus in the Gospel of Luke, edited by D. A. Carson and Kathleen B. Nielson (2015)

The Scriptures Testify about Me: Jesus and the Gospel in the Old Testament, edited by D. A. Carson (2013)

Word-Filled Women's Ministry: Loving and Serving the Church, edited by Gloria Furman and Kathleen B. Nielson (2015)

Joyfully Spreading
the Word

Sharing the Good News of Jesus

Kathleen Nielson and Gloria Furman,
editors

WHEATON, ILLINOIS

Trade paperback ISBN: 978-1-4335-5943-3
ePub ISBN: 978-1-4335-5946-4
PDF ISBN: 978-1-4335-5944-0
Mobipocket ISBN: 978-1-4335-5945-7

Library of Congress Cataloging-in-Publication Data

Names: Nielson, Kathleen Buswell, editor. | Furman, Gloria, 1980- editor.
Title: Joyfully spreading the word : sharing the good news of Jesus / Kathleen Nielson and Gloria Furman, editors.
Description: Wheaton, Illinois : Crossway, [2018] | Series: The gospel coalition | Includes bibliographical references and index.
Identifiers: LCCN 2017048084 (print) | LCCN 2018015600 (ebook) | ISBN 9781433559440 (pdf) | ISBN 9781433559457 (mobi) | ISBN 9781433559464 (epub) | ISBN 9781433559433 (trade paperback) | ISBN 9781433559464 (ePub)
Subjects: LCSH: Witness bearing (Christianity) | Women in Christianity.
Classification: LCC BV4520 (ebook) | LCC BV4520 .J69 2018 (print) | DDC 248/.5--dc23
LC record available at https://lccn.loc.gov/2017048084

Crossway is a publishing ministry of Good News Publishers.

BP		28	27	26	25	24	23	22	21	20	19	18
15	14	13	12	11	10	9	8	7	6	5	4	3	2	1

To the women in this volume whose names have been changed
or left out to protect their privacy—
those who have received the gift of faith in Christ Jesus,
and those we pray will yet believe,
those who have been spreading the good news for years,
and those who have only just begun.
Oh, the stories of grace being woven around the globe,
stories we shall spend eternity unraveling, with joy,
together giving glory to our Savior.

.

Contents

Oh, magnify the LᴊORD with me,
and let us exalt his name together!

Psalm 34:3

Introduction

Kathleen Nielson

This is a book by women and mainly for women—but certainly not all about women. It's about the gospel and sharing the gospel—making known the good news that God has redeemed us sinners through the death and resurrection of his Son, the Lord Jesus Christ, in whom we are called to believe and find life. As women in the church learn and grow together, following Paul's instruction to Titus that older women should teach the younger ones "what is good" (Titus 2:3), a call to evangelism must be a crucial part of the good things passed on. Although it is clearly the concern of the whole church, the subject of sharing the gospel is one that women will do well to consider deeply together. Let me suggest three specific reasons why.

1. EVANGELISM TURNS US OUTWARD

First, believing women need to hear voices calling us to a gospel-centered outward focus—rather than a self-centered, inward one. Especially in Western contexts where many Christians have lived comfortably for a long time, there is often a lack of passion and clarity about communicating the gospel to those who don't know Christ. I regularly find a great deal of passion among women for personal issues, amid the challenges of relatively well-to-do lives that can leave us stressed or lazy or worried about physical appearances or tempted by easily available, ungodly entertainment. It is easy for many of us to focus on inward-oriented questions that are important but that can fill our thoughts: questions about self-image and identity, emotional health, finding just the right work and finding satisfaction in that work, etc. When we do turn outward toward social issues and actions—and, happily, we increasingly do—the temptation is to turn with passion to the physical and emotional needs that move our hearts. Why are we not equally moved, or even more moved, to share the good news of Jesus and how he can meet the greatest and eternal needs of every needy human being?

Questions concerning sharing the good news of Jesus need not cancel out other, more inward questions. A focus on the gospel and the power of the gospel inevitably feeds our own souls in remarkable ways. At the Gospel Coalition's 2016 National Women's Conference, a workshop panel assembled to discuss the topic, "Evangelism: Sharing the Reason for Our Hope."[1] The panel brought together women who minister in universities and neighborhoods and cross-cultural settings—but, most important, it brought together women on whose lips is regularly the good news of what God has done for us in Jesus Christ. Their hearts for the gospel came through, not in a theoretical way, but with loving care for the people around them who have not received the gift of eternal life in Christ. Their hearts for the Lord himself came through; it was clear that in sharing the Lord Jesus, they had come to know and love him even more deeply and securely. We heard these voices on the panel calling us to evangelism, and we knew it would be good to hear more.

2. EVANGELISM THRIVES ON ROLE MODELS

We're already talking about the second reason women should be considering together the subject of personal evangelism: there are great role models who can teach us biblically and well. For many years, Rebecca Manley Pippert has served as a wonderful public role model; with her classic book *Out of the Salt Shaker*, Becky helped shake many of us awake to the beauty and the real possibility of talking with people about Jesus and seeing them drawn by God to faith. What confirms the goodness of Becky's model is that she has continued powerfully to inspire many on this subject, serving in recent decades more internationally than in her native United States. I'm grateful she has agreed to join us in this volume on a subject she has lived out personally and with faithful perseverance.

Such role models, of course, speak not only to women. And, indeed, such public role models must join a host of private ones, so that we will all know we're part of a family enterprise, a whole prayerful purpose of the body of Christ to see the church grow by adding new believers. But it is true that women can play a significant part in this enterprise in a myriad of ways—and one way is through offering role models to the next generation, to help them envision just what a woman with a heart to share the gospel looks like in action. We're hoping that the voices in this book will offer some helpful role models and inspire a whole lot more.

The contributors are women simply serving in the places where God put them, showing and sharing the good news of what God has done to save us through his Son. Many of these women juggle a variety of contexts, mixing home and work and friendship and hospitality and mercy ministry in that sometimes-chaotic combination that makes up many women's lives. We hope the multiple involvements highlighted by these women will spur others on to see that we can share the gospel from any and every life context, from a kitchen table to an office desk to a podium in front of thousands. We hope these women's stories will stimulate creative thinking concerning the possibility of reaching out not just to people across the globe but to neighbors across the street and people across town. Speaking of stories—we hope you enjoy them; there are a lot of compelling stories in this book, and just *telling* them turned out to be one of the most effective means of lighting up the subject of evangelism in a most personal way.

We also hope these voices will spur us on to increasingly careful, consistent study of God's Word—not simply in order to feed ourselves, but also to feed others with the Word of truth. The contributors to this volume are women who have immersed themselves deeply in the Scriptures. Their thoughts and words are full of God's Word. Their articulations of clear gospel apologetics grow from the very logic and flow of the Old and New Testaments, with Jesus at the center of the story. They would remind us that it is the Word of God that makes people wise for salvation (2 Tim. 3:15). They call us to trust this Word as the sword of the Spirit, and they provide heartening examples of what it looks like to wield this sword with excellence, humility, and trust in God alone for the salvation of those he calls. Hearing these women's voices will help transform our picture of Bible study from that of a routine meal to an ever-larger table where we get to share an amazing feast.

3. EVANGELISM IS URGENT

Third, and finally, women should be considering deeply together the subject of personal evangelism because we sense the urgency of teaching each other this part of "what is good." The paragraph immediately following Paul's instructions to Titus concerning the various groups within the church gives the big reason for all his instructions:

> For the grace of God has appeared, bringing salvation for all people, training us to renounce ungodliness and worldly passions, and to live self-controlled, upright, and godly lives in the present age, waiting for our blessed hope, the appearing of the glory of our great God and Savior Jesus Christ. (Titus 2:11–13)

The emphasis in this passage is God's redemptive work through Jesus Christ that has come for "all people," and that happens in a certain time frame—a time frame that will culminate in the second coming of the Lord Jesus to earth, in all his glory.

What Paul calls the "present age" is the same period also referred to in Scripture as the "last days" (Acts 2:17; Heb. 1:2). These terms describe the time in which we now live—the time between Jesus's first and second coming. It's a time of taking salvation to all the nations, as believers spread the good news, until Jesus's return. According to his clear command before he left the earth, Jesus's calling of believers during this time is to "go . . . and make disciples of all nations, baptizing them in the name of the Father and of the Son and of the Holy Spirit, teaching them to observe all that I have commanded you" (Matt. 28:18–20).

That command was given to Jesus's disciples and is passed on through them to the church, with its preachers and teachers and evangelists who lead the church in making and teaching disciples both near and far. This volume's contributors love and depend on the context of the church, and specifically local congregations, for the work of the Great Commission. (Watch for how many of their stories make local churches a part of the action!) This book celebrates participation in the Great Commission by every single church member, under the leadership of pastors and elders. And this book in particular encourages women to feel the urgency of this call, just as did the women in the early church. Just think of all those fellow female workers mentioned by Paul: Phoebe, Prisca, Mary, Junia, Tryphaena and Tryphosa, Persis, Rufus's mother, Julia, and Nereus's sister (see Romans 16).

Among people who enjoy all the economic progress and technological enlightenment of the twenty-first century, rather than urgency there can be even a slight embarrassment about the simple truth that the Bible lights up the way to salvation through Jesus. That Jesus is the Christ, the Son of God who died for us, bearing our sins and suffering the wrath of God in our place; that he rose from the grave, providing eternal life for all who believe in him—

this is indeed the good and relatively simple news the Bible teaches and Christians get to share. We share it today in a time when the church is growing fast all over the globe, even in nations that are politically "closed" but where King Jesus is at work through his people and his Word (and through some of the women writing here). It is urgent news indeed, as the hope of Jesus's coming draws ever nearer.

CALLED TO FAITH AND CALLED TO SHARE IT

Co-editor Gloria Furman and I are praying that this book will further the conversation among women concerning this call to share the good news of Jesus. We all need voices calling us to a gospel-centered outward focus. We need strong, Word-filled role models. And we need a sense of the urgency of this message, this message that calls people from death to life through the power of the gospel. This is the bread of life that lasts forever, and we need to share it.

The women writing in this book have greatly encouraged me, and I hope they will encourage you. They come from different cultures, denominations, age groups, family situations, and backgrounds. And from all those spots where God has placed them, they are reaching out with the gospel. I can do this too, and so can you, by God's grace. God has reached into the life of every believer, calling each one to himself by the Spirit, through faith in Christ—and then calling each one to give testimony to that faith to those around them, until Jesus comes again.

These women all celebrate the fact that it is God who does the calling, from start to finish. That is the joyful confidence these chapters exude. God calls us by his Spirit and according to his Word, to faith in Christ—who is with us always, to the end of the age.

PART 1

CORE CONCERNS

1

The Glorious *What* of Evangelism

Becky Pippert

The gospel of Jesus Christ is the most glorious, liberating news that has ever graced our weary, battered planet. Just before the resurrected Jesus ascended into heaven he commanded his disciples to share this good news, and that command extends to all of his followers—in our towns, our communities, and to the ends of the earth. His instructions have nothing to do with our gifts or personality types! He simply commanded, "Therefore go and make disciples of all nations" (Matt. 28:19 NIV; cf. Acts 1:8). The best decision anyone anywhere can ever make, in response to God's grace, is to become a disciple of Jesus Christ—by faith in his death on the cross in our place and his resurrection from the dead that promises eternal life. Nothing is more important. Nothing.

The cultural landscape can seem daunting to those who would share this good news—especially those in the Western world. Many pundits and analysts say that America in particular is moving in the direction of secular Europe. The Christian church is growing dramatically in other parts of the globe—but not so much in the West, where, with the impact of advanced modernity, influential voices are becoming increasingly hostile and antagonistic to true Christian faith. Today any statement of biblical truth about God is often seen as arrogant, intolerant, and politically incorrect.

But a truth-denying culture doesn't have the power to take away people's longing for meaning and worth. If anything, it exacerbates it. God has placed in all human beings the longing for identity, purpose, and relationship, even if people can't quite articulate what they feel they are missing. Yet how will unbelievers know where to look unless Christians both live and tell the good news of what God has done for us in Christ?

Still, our present culture poses increasing challenges for the gospel. For example, I recently had a conversation with a woman who said, "I believe we must honor the god who dwells within our psyche and trust our hearts to guide us—and Oprah really agrees with me!"

A "New Age" devotee[1] told me she no longer believes in the Christian God (if she ever did) because God hadn't answered her prayers for her sister's recovery from cancer: "When she died, I knew I had to find a belief system that deifies the human self, so I could exercise greater control." I asked her if she was experiencing any challenges in her New Age faith: "Well," she said, "I haven't quite grasped how to fully apprehend my deity—I think that's why I'm not seeing the answers I want."

Another woman told me that she was a convinced atheist and that life had no meaning: "Human beings are nothing more than meaningless pieces of protoplasm. There is no God—which Darwin has so clearly proven."

Christianity, of course, says something altogether different. Even though a great deal of the Christian message runs counter to our culture, we can still respond intelligently, persuasively, and winsomely to people with very different views. However, if we don't understand *what* we believe, we won't be persuasive in communicating our faith to others.

In my years as an evangelist, and as my husband and I have given evangelism training to believers all over the world, we have learned that the deepest motivation for witness comes by first understanding what we believe. It is our *theology* that must impact our *methodology*. Not to overlook the importance of the *how*—but it's absolutely vital that we begin with the *what*. Never has this been truer than today, for in a truth-denying world, even Christians are tempted to lose confidence in the powerful truth of the gospel. This truth is personal truth: in understanding the *what* of our faith, we come to know more deeply and speak more clearly about the one in whom our faith rests.

How do we discover truth about who God is and what he has done for us in Christ? The Judeo-Christian faith is based not on what we think about God, but on what God has revealed about himself: *Christianity is a religion of revelation.* God has made himself known in many ways, but his primary revelation is through his written Word, the Bible, which reveals the Word made flesh: Jesus the Son of God. When we give testimony to our faith, we are sharing not just our own experience but our experience of God's life-changing revelation to us in Christ.

So let's follow the biblical storyline of that revelation: *Creation—Crisis—Christ's Redemption—Christ's Return.*

THE CREATOR GOD AND A GOOD CREATION

In a world filled with multiple-choice starting points, we must start where the Bible starts: "In the beginning God . . ." (Gen. 1:1). In Genesis 1–2, we discover a great deal about who God is:

- *God is eternal and sovereign*: God is without beginning or end, having no peer or competitor. God has absolute authority. He commanded and it was accomplished.

- *God is the Creator*: He created all things out of nothing; he needed no help. That God created the world means he is above and beyond all he has made, and is distinct from it.
- *God is good*: His character is righteous and holy, loving and merciful, trustworthy and faithful.
- *God is personal and communicative*: God is not some distant, impersonal power—or a detached mind—or an energy field. God is a loving, personal God who delights and shows parental, nurturing concern over what he creates.

This God created human beings as the apex of his entire creation—all finally declared by him to be "very good" (Gen. 1:31). What made human beings unique from all the rest of creation is that only humans were created in the image of God. Adam and Eve were given language, creativity, love, holiness, immortality, and freedom (within divine limits) to choose their actions. They were created to love and know God, to live in harmony with him and the rest of creation, to reveal God to the rest of his creation, and to rule the world as God's stewards, under his sovereign, loving rule. This is our crucial starting point as we interact and share the good news with others: every single human being is created by God in the image of God.

Everything God created was made for God's glory and for human benefit. Adam and Eve had an open, intimate relationship with God; a loving relationship with each other; fulfilling work to do; and a world full of pleasures, tastes, sights, and smells! They were created to enjoy God's goodness and submit to God's gracious will. All of Eden was given to them with only one restriction: "You are free to eat from any tree in the garden; but you must not eat from the tree of the knowledge of good and evil, for when you eat from it you will certainly die" (Gen. 2:16–17). God placed the tree in the center of the garden and clearly warned Adam and Eve of the consequence if they willfully chose *independence* instead of *God-dependence*: They would surely die.

But the principal feature of life—*life as God intended*—was a lavish gift. *The gospel message from start to finish is God's personal offer of amazing grace!*

CRISIS: THE FALL AND THE MESS WE MADE OF THINGS

People around us today often scoff at the notion of sin. Our world has new names for what ails us: poor self-esteem, neurosis, addiction, anxiety, psychological wounding, etc. It isn't that these issues are not a reality; it's that such analysis does not go deep enough to reveal the root cause.

Yet for all the protest that sin is an old-fashioned, outdated concept, nearly everyone agrees that something has gone terribly wrong and must be made right. We see the wrong in world wars, racism, genocides, terrorism, human trafficking, exploitation of children—and in our own personal battles evidenced in broken relationships, anger, addictions, and on and on.

What happened that caused our planet to go from paradise to our present brokenness? In Genesis 3, we discover that, though Adam and Eve were created in God's image, they rejected God's rule and chose to be self-ruled when they disobeyed God's command not to eat the fruit of that tree. As a result, sin entered the human race: there is now no area of human personhood that is not infected by sin—even though we still reflect, however dimly, the image of God in which each human being is made. But the perfection God had established was broken, and human beings have been in the grip of sin ever since, as Genesis 4–11 so chillingly describes. Sin is such an all-inclusive reality on our planet that Paul says: "For all have sinned and fall short of the glory of God" (Rom. 3:23). Like Adam and Eve, all humans have chosen self-rule instead of God-rule.

That means that everything we see around us and in us that is so tragically wrong—natural disasters, famine, genocides, and all forms of personal brokenness—can be traced back to the time when human beings first rebelled against God. Into that garden came the evil Serpent, whom Revelation identifies as "that ancient serpent, who is the devil, or Satan" (Rev. 20:2). The Bible reveals the reality of Satan and other supernatural beings who have rebelled against God and who do their best to tempt human beings to sin. Although the Bible reveals various forms of evil, such as corporate systemic evil and Satan and his demons—the Bible is clear that at the heart of sin is personal rebellion against God.

Genesis 3: Sin's Essence and Sin's Outcome

Over dinner, a skeptic psychiatrist friend described the typical problems that drive people to seek her help. Then she said: "But you're a Christian, so you think the problem is that we're all sinners!" I asked what she thought the biblical understanding of sin was, and she answered, "Oh, something along the lines of drugs, sex, and rock 'n roll?"

What my friend didn't grasp is that from the biblical perspective, sin at its core isn't just misdeeds. The Bible locates sin at the very center of human personality. Sin could be described as having a *God-complex*: we get ourselves and God mixed up! We live as if we are in charge. Sin is actually twofold: it's the deliberate refusal to trust and worship God as God, and it's the prideful claim to insist on the right to run our lives. Sin is both unbelief and idolatry, as we try to create meaning and identity by depending on things other than God.

Biblically speaking, sin is always against God. That is why we can't understand sin's true meaning without understanding that sin, first and foremost, is rebellion and disobedience against a righteous God.

What was the final outcome of human disobedience to God? When Adam and Eve turned away from God in rebellion, God declared to them his righteous judgment, just as he had promised. Suffering and death fell upon the human race. The consequence of Adam and Eve's rebellion was disastrous: the human race became catastrophically separated from the eternal love of God. The perfect trust and warm, intimate friendship they had enjoyed with God and with each other were destroyed; they lived instead under his judgment of death. God's presence was removed and human beings experienced a spiritual separation from God they had never known.

The predicament of fallen humanity is so serious, so grave, and so desperately wrong from within and without, that it is beyond human ability to fix. Think about it: Can fallen human beings change the intrinsic structure of our sinful nature and remake our natures from the inside? Can we defeat Satan? Do we have the power to conquer death? Clearly we do not!

Who then has the power to deliver and rescue us? Who can take what is so terribly wrong and make it right? Obviously, only a power that is stronger than ourselves can help us overcome ourselves. Nothing short of divine intervention can rectify our situation.

We glimpse this divine intervention even in the garden of Eden. Although God banished Adam and Eve from the garden, he didn't stop loving them, as we see when he tenderly made them better clothes than what they'd made for themselves, to protect them once they were outside the garden.

Most important, in Genesis 3:14–15, God declares war on the Serpent (Satan) and says that the offspring of the woman will crush the Serpent's head. The whole rest of the Old Testament points toward the coming of that promised offspring who would finally defeat Satan: Jesus the Savior, born of a woman named Mary. God will not allow the Enemy's plan to harm his plan. This is the first promise of the gospel!

The Bible reveals that before the beginning of time and the human revolt, God had already decided on his plan of how to rescue the planet that had turned from him (Titus 1:2; Eph. 3:11). He would send a Redeemer, Christ Jesus the divine Son of God, who would endure suffering and death in order to bring sinners back to God. *Even in human rebellion we see the promise of God's grace.*

CHRIST AND OUR REDEMPTION

The good news of the gospel is that sin and judgment were not the end of the story!

Though God owed us nothing, in his mercy and grace he sent his divine Son from heaven on a rescue mission in order to redeem a people for himself and to restore everything under Christ: "to bring unity to all things in heaven and on earth under Christ" (Eph. 1:10).

How did the Father send his Son? Christ Jesus came to us from heaven through his birth, life and ministry, death and resurrection, and ascension. What theologians call the doctrine of the incarnation affirms that Jesus was the God-man: his nature was fully divine and fully human, though without sin. While each aspect of Jesus's life has vital lessons in evangelism, we must focus on the cross and resurrection to grasp the heart of this good news we have to share.

The Death of Jesus

It is extraordinary to realize what Jesus's death accomplished: human rebellion and sin were overcome, the power of the enemy was conquered, and death was defeated. While all that Christ's death accomplished is vitally important, it is the overcoming of sin that lies at the very heart of the meaning of the crucifixion.

What we often miss is how a holy and loving God could forgive sin without compromising his holiness—and yet judge evil without frustrating his love. What is God to do? He loves us and we have rebelled. His nature is loving, but he is also just. Someone once told me, "I believe in Karma! The law of Karma is harsh: *you sin—and you pay!* It's as simple as that!"

But the amazing good news of the gospel is this: *you sin—and God paid!* When the just judgment of a holy God had to fall, Christ became our substitute, and the wrath of God fell on him. It is a remarkable fact: we are the proud sinners, but the final sacrifice for our sin and pride is God, a willing victim.

The late John Stott wrote:

For the essence of sin is man substituting himself for God, while the essence of salvation is God substituting himself for man. Man asserts himself against God and puts himself where only God deserves to be; God sacrifices himself for man and put himself where only man deserves to be. Man claims prerogatives which belong to God alone; God accepts penalties which belong to man alone.[2]

We can never humanly fathom what Jesus endured on the cross. We get a hint in the garden of Gethsemane when we see Jesus's profound sorrow as he realized what he was about to face on the cross (Matt. 26:36–46; Luke 22:39–46). But the deepest clue is hearing Jesus's loud cry from the cross: "My God, my God, why have you forsaken me?" (Matt. 27:46). Now we see a glimpse of the cost Jesus endured: "God made him who had no sin to be sin for us, so that in him we might become the righteousness of God" (2 Cor. 5:21). At the cross Jesus took on himself the sins of the whole world—from all nations, past, present, and future—bearing God's wrath as the perfect and final sacrifice for all who believe in him (1 John 2:2, 23–25). Just as sin separates us from God's presence, so Jesus was separated from the very presence of God.

That, far more than the nails and suffocation, is why the cross was so excruciating. To pay the price for human sin, Jesus had to experience the utter anguish and abandonment of being separated from God and bearing his judgment for sin. That is what hell is, to be severed from God's presence and under God's wrath; *hell is what Jesus's agony was about.* Christ had never known a moment apart from the presence of his Father until the cross.

In light of this, there is only one question before us: *What kind of God willingly sacrifices everything so that he can be in relationship with his creation?* Remember, God the Father didn't start loving us *after* Jesus went to the cross. God's love for us sent him there. The cross didn't procure grace; it flowed from grace. Christ took our sinfulness into himself and overcame in his own heart what could not be overcome in human life. That is why the cross is the dividing line of human history. In every facet of God's action on the cross we see divine love at work. *More than any other act of human history, the cross reveals why the good news of Jesus Christ is truly a gospel of grace.*

The Resurrection of Jesus

How do we know that God accepted the sacrifice of Christ? How can we be sure that our estranged human race can now be reconciled to God? Because Jesus Christ arose from the dead! The resurrection and Christ's freshly healed wounds are the proof that God has accepted Jesus's sacrifice for us.

The wounds that the risen Jesus showed his disciples represented his suffering and death on the cross, his gift of love (Luke 24:36–40). When Jesus told them, "Peace be with you," he was offering real peace, because through his wounds and resurrected life we can now be reconciled to God as we put our faith in him. This is the message of the gospel that we are called and privileged to share.

We don't share this gospel in our own strength. Just before the risen Jesus ascended into heaven, he promised the disciples that he would send them (and, by implication, every believer from that time forward) the gift of the Holy Spirit—the very presence of the risen Christ with us and in us (John 14:15–17, 25–26). Then he commissioned them (and us) to go out into the world and share the gospel. Now, because of the Holy Spirit's presence in our lives, all believers are empowered and strengthened to be witnesses for the Lord Jesus who died for our sins and rose again, reconciling us to God forever.

Jesus didn't come to earth to make good people better but to give life to the dead! Through the cross and resurrection, God in Christ Jesus forgives the guilt of our sin, frees us from the enslavement of sin, gives us a new nature through the power of the Holy Spirit, and promises us eternal life! What gifts for those who believe! This is good news indeed! Beginning to grasp the amazing *what* of our faith indeed spurs us on to share it with others who desperately need to know how to find life, as opposed to death.

CHRIST'S RETURN: RESTORATION

Even the glory of all that Christ accomplished through his death and resurrection isn't the end of the gospel story. The Bible shouts from the rooftops that Jesus came to reconcile the world to God— *and* that he will come again! All of human history is moving toward that God-appointed goal. The personal return of Jesus Christ will end human history as we know it, ushering in a new and endless age, and completing God's eternal plan for salvation.

When Jesus first came to earth, he ushered in the kingdom of heaven, but he didn't erase all the effects of sin on our planet. Human beings would still experience hardship, injustice, disease, and death. It is only when Christ returns and brings the presence of heaven with him, that all forms of evil—sin, Satan, and death—will be destroyed forever and he will make all things new.

I heard a remarkable sermon by pastor and theologian Peter Lewis in Nottingham, England, on the four significant events that will take place at Christ's return:[3]

(1) *There will be a reckoning.* The Bible says that at the end of history the dead from every generation will be raised from death and Christ will judge all who have ever lived (John 5:28–29; 3:18, 36). There will be justice at last because God will rectify all wrongs and establish his righteous rule forever. Those who have refused God's offer of grace and who tragically insist on living apart from God's presence will in effect have their request honored. The Bible is clear that God wants no one to perish, but everyone to come to repentance (2 Pet. 3:9). The Bible is also clear that God, through Christ Jesus, will judge all humankind fairly (Rom. 2:11). While this is hard for people to hear in our age of tolerance, those who have rejected God "will be punished with everlasting destruction

and shut out from the presence of the Lord and from the glory of his might" (2 Thess. 1:9).

The Bible presents this judgment both as God's sovereign, holy will and also as human beings' choice. C. S. Lewis illumines the perspective of human choice:

> There are only two kinds of people in the end: those who say to God, "Thy will be done," and those to whom God says, in the end, "*Thy* will be done." All that are in Hell, choose it. . . . No soul that seriously and constantly desires joy will ever miss it. Those who seek, find. To those who knock it is opened.[4]

Christians need not approach Jesus's judgment with fear. The Judge we meet on the day of judgment is the Jesus who loves us and the one we have known and loved in this life (Rom. 8:1). No wonder Paul looked forward to rejoicing at Christ's coming with those to whom he'd preached the gospel and who had believed (1 Thess. 2:19)!

(2) *There will be a reunion with Jesus.* Everyone, friend or foe and from every generation, will see Jesus when he returns to earth. To be clear, for believers who die *before* Christ's return, there will be reunion with the Lord Jesus in heaven, just as he told the thief on the cross (Luke 23:42–43). But even though life in heaven now is joyous, it is still temporary. Only at Christ's return will we see the full culmination of human history. First there is the judgment, and then Jesus will set up God's kingdom on earth: "God's dwelling place is now among the people, and he will dwell with them. They will be his people, and God himself will be with them and be their God" (Rev. 21:3).

(3) *There will be a resurrection for all believers.* When Christ returns, we will receive our resurrected bodies, just as Jesus did at his resurrection. We will enjoy a world where loved ones no longer die and where there are no more tears or sorrow or hurt—just the supreme blessing of being with the Lord God (1 Cor. 15:52–54).

(4) *There will be renewal.* There will be a healing and restoration of our planet! Jesus will renew the whole earth and heaven. We will find ourselves in our own but renewed bodies, and in a renewed earth and heaven.

GOOD NEWS THAT MUST BE SHARED!

Why does the good news of Jesus Christ fill us with hope and joy? Because evil doesn't have the last word—God does! Satan will be led to his doom and God's people will be united to God and to each other, for the old will have gone and the new will be here. A great part of the witness of God's people is that we are filled with this hope, even in the midst of the greatest suffering.

What do we do while we wait for Christ's return? We are living in the period of history between Christ's first and second coming. It is the "already and not yet" phase of human history. What are we to do? We pray for Christ's return and we work for God's glory!

At the heart of our prayer and work must be the spread of God's glory through the spread of the gospel of his Son. As followers of Jesus Christ, we must be passionately committed to evangelism through witness that is *visual* (through our being and our deeds) and *verbal*. Biblical evangelism always involves both aspects, not just one! Our approach to evangelism must be biblically faithful, culturally relevant, spiritually empowered, and relationally effective. Above all, we must love as Christ has loved us: "Because we loved you so much, we were delighted to share with you not only the gospel of God but our lives as well" (1 Thess. 2:8).

As we share our lives, we won't share all at once this amazing *what* of the gospel that this chapter has begun to unfold. We'll ask questions of our friends and acquaintances; we'll be ready to answer when people ask about our hope (1 Pet. 3:15); we'll pray and we'll sense when someone is ready to hear more. But as we ourselves more and more fully grasp the theology of our faith—the *what* and the *who*—then our questions and our answers will be more and more clear. We'll be spurred on and enabled by the Holy Spirit to bear faithful witness, as God's Word dwells richly in us.

God wants to use us! We do not have the power to produce conversions in others—nor can we make people see their sin; that power belongs to God alone. So we share our lives and the good news of Jesus with our fellow image bearers, praying that a sense of sin and an awareness of their need for the gospel will be awakened through the Holy Spirit. And, as God graciously enables, we will have the profound privilege and thrill of helping people commit their lives to Christ Jesus as they repent and believe in him.

Jesus commands all believers to "go and make disciples of all nations" (Matt. 28:19). When we see the beauty and glory of the gospel, the victory won by the Son of God on our behalf and in our place, and the cosmic significance of all that Christ has accomplished, how can we possibly remain silent and keep this glorious news to ourselves?

2

The Heart of the Evangelist

Megan Hill

"Secure your own oxygen mask first before assisting other passengers."

This directive is familiar to anyone who has traveled in recent years on a commercial airplane. In the event of an emergency ("a sudden loss of cabin pressure"), we are told that an oxygen mask would descend from the plane's ceiling for each person. Naturally, in such a scary moment, mothers would instinctively try to get the air to their children first, husbands and wives would want to ensure that their beloved spouses could breathe, and adult children would focus on preserving the life of elderly parents seated next to them. Such altruism might be instinctive but it is not wise, the airlines warn. A passenger who is herself wheezing is in no condition to rescue others. If she passes out from lack of oxygen, neither she nor her helpless seatmates will survive.

In our efforts to share the gospel, we should take counsel from the flight attendants. We are in an emergency situation: all around us, people are gasping for spiritual breath. But in order to best assist them, we must have our own supply firmly affixed. Nearly one hundred years before the advent of commercial air travel, Scottish pastor Robert Murray M'Cheyne wrote similar counsel to a brother in Christ: "Take heed to thyself. Your own soul is your first and greatest care. You know a sound body alone can work with power, much more a healthy soul."[1] And nearly two thousand years before M'Cheyne, the apostle Paul wrote to Timothy with these words: "Keep a close watch on yourself and on the teaching. Persist in this, for by so doing you will save both yourself and your hearers" (1 Tim. 4:16). If you want to labor effectively for Christ, secure your own soul's oxygen mask first.

The voices in this book call us to consider the biblical imperative of evangelism, the substance of the gospel good news, and the ways in which God by his Spirit enables us to share that news in all the callings and contexts of our lives. The evangelistic task appears before us with both urgency and privilege: the fields are ready for harvest (John 4:35), the nations are surging toward Zion (Mic. 4:2), the mystery of Christ has now been revealed (Col. 1:26–27), and today is the day of salvation (2 Cor. 6:2).

Now is the time for evangelism. And so now is the time to consider the state of our own souls. By diligently preparing our hearts, we will be stirred to begin the evangelistic task, made sensitive to the needs around us, and equipped to persevere through inevitable days of discouragement. We will also store up the rich gospel content that is the essential hope we offer our dead and dying neighbors.[2]

In this chapter, then, we will strap on our own oxygen masks before forging ahead to the particular contexts in which helpless souls need our attention. And what is our vital preparation for evangelism? We are going to consider four things: (1) a personal, substantive knowledge of Christ, (2) a habit of fervent prayer, (3) the diligent practice of holiness, and (4) a public commitment to the life of the local church. To cultivate in ourselves the heart of an evangelist, we must take up nothing less than the whole Christian life.

KNOWING CHRIST

As people who share the gospel, our first and most essential resource is not something we can secure for ourselves. Instead, someone else secured it for us. While we were yet sinners, while we were enemies and strangers to God, while we were far off and lost and blind and ignorant and dead, Christ died for us. By his life of perfect obedience, his death on the cross, and his resurrection from the grave, Christ secured our relationship with the triune God. Christ freed us from the power and guilt of our sin, and then, as J. Todd Billings explains, "We . . . enter into the playful, joyous world of *living as children of a gracious Father, as persons united to Christ and empowered by the Spirit.*"[3]

You may have come to know Christ early in your childhood—encouraged by godly parents and taught by loving Sunday school teachers. You may have come to know him when you were a teenager—invited to a youth group or campus ministry by your Christian friend. You may have come as an adult—wooed out of years of wandering by the words of a lone preacher or of a hundred preachers. You may have met Christ when you were obviously rebellious or when you were seemingly upstanding. You may have met Christ in a crowded worship service or in the solitude of your own bedroom. You may have met him suddenly and unexpectedly or as the inevitable answer to your persistent questions. But somewhere along the way, believer, you met Jesus. And you have not been the same since.

Knowing Christ—loving him, worshiping him, meditating on him, enjoying him, and becoming more like him—is the primary resource every evangelist must have. It is because of our own personal experience with Christ that we invite others to meet him too. Like Philip, we have been found by Christ, and so we hurry to find others (John 1:46). Like the woman at the well, we have heard the voice of Jesus, and so we speak to others (John 4:29). Like Paul, we affirm, "I know whom I have believed" (2 Tim. 1:12), and like Peter and John, we insist, "We cannot but speak of what we have seen and heard" (Acts 4:20).

Several times a year, I find an email in my inbox that reads like this: "I've been asked to introduce you as the speaker at our upcoming event. Would you please tell me some things about you that I can say in my introduction?" The sender of that email always has my sympathy—she has been given a very difficult task. In just a few words, she must communicate to her hearers my value as a conference speaker and pique their eagerness to learn from my teaching. And she has never actually met me.

Thankfully, this is not our situation as evangelists! We are not simply arranging a few quick facts about Jesus that we can use to introduce him to others. We introduce Christ to others out of our deep personal knowledge of him—the beloved friend who delivered us from the kingdom of darkness and brought us into his marvelous light (1 Pet. 2:9). This connection between our own experiential knowledge of Christ and our impulse to share Christ with others is clearly seen in David's familiar psalm of repentance:[4]

Have mercy on me, O God,
   according to your steadfast love;
according to your abundant mercy
   blot out my transgressions.
Wash me thoroughly from my iniquity,
   and cleanse me from my sin! . . .
Create in me a clean heart, O God,
   and renew a right spirit within me.
Cast me not away from your presence,
   and take not your Holy Spirit from me.
Restore to me the joy of your salvation,
   and uphold me with a willing spirit.

> *Then I will teach transgressors your ways,*
> *and sinners will return to you.* (Ps. 51:1–2, 10–13)

Having known the weight of his own sin ("my sin is ever before me," v. 3) and having received the joy of salvation (v. 12), David resolves to teach others what he has himself learned by experience. David's testimony of grace becomes the content of his evangelism. The same is true for us. Has Christ saved you from the just judgment for your sin? Has he delighted you with his loveliness and revived you with his Word? Has he bound you to himself and given you his Spirit? Has he joined you to his church and met with you in worship? Has he sympathized with you, prayed for you, and made you more like himself, day after day? Then you already have everything you need to introduce him to your neighbors.

But there is a second dimension of our knowledge of Christ. It's true that we don't merely know Christ as a list of facts about him, but we nevertheless do seek to know about him. Just as a wife takes care to learn about her husband or a mother about her children—What do they enjoy? What do they dislike? What have their past experiences been? What are their desires for the future?—we make it a point to learn all we can about Christ. And we learn this in the pages of the Bible.

"The grand primary object of all Scripture is to testify of Jesus,"[5] wrote J. C. Ryle. Every part of the Bible—each event and person, each law and prophecy, each parable and exhortation—reveals something about Christ to us. If we want to know Christ better, we will be diligent in studying the Bible. We will read and memorize it in private. We will discuss it in our homes with our families and guests. We will eagerly learn from it as it is read and preached in the public worship of the church. At every opportunity, we will be students of the Word.

This knowledge then fuels evangelism. As Al Mohler put it: "Evangelism is dependent on words."[6] In evangelism, we use precise ideas and logical arguments to communicate gospel truth to our neighbors. We pause in the break room and linger at the campus mailboxes and sit for a moment at a child's bedside—and we speak. So in order to have adequate words ready on our tongues, we need to store them up in our hearts. Jesus himself reminded us, "Out of the abundance of the heart the mouth speaks" (Matt. 12:34) and "The good person out of the good treasure of his heart produces good" (Luke 6:45). The evangelist's heart must be filled with Scripture so that its overflow will be a constant proclamation of the good news of Christ crucified for sinners.

A thorough knowledge of Christ in the Scriptures will also equip us to answer our neighbors' questions and objections. Scripture is "breathed out by God and profitable for teaching, for reproof, for correction, and for training in righteousness, that the man of God may be complete, equipped for every good work" (2 Tim. 3:16–17). What confidence this gives us! No matter how powerless we feel in the face of our neighbors' persistent opposition, we have stored in our hearts the very thing to overcome stubborn souls. When we evangelize, we present God's powerful Word, "the sacred writings, which are able to make you wise for salvation through faith in Christ Jesus" (2 Tim. 3:15).

Knowing Christ personally and substantively is the first resource of the evangelist's heart. When we meditate on the work of Christ in our own lives and when we learn more about Christ in the pages of the Bible, we overflow with the good news of Christ to our neighbors. As Matthew Henry wrote, "Penitents should be preachers; those that have taken warning themselves to turn and live should give warning to others not to go on and die."[7]

PRAYER

The second resource of the evangelist's heart is prayer. In prayer, we approach the loving Father through the interceding Son with the help of the pleading Spirit (Rom. 8:15–17, 26–27, 33–39). As believers, it is our duty to pray ("Pray without ceasing," 1 Thess. 5:17), and it is our privilege to pray ("Let us then with confidence draw near to the throne of grace," Heb. 4:16). Though outwardly unremarkable, our prayers are a spiritual weapon in a spiritual war (Eph. 6:10–20), a weapon God uses to accomplish both judgment (Rev. 8:3–5) and salvation (2 Cor. 1:11). And by the prayers of his people, God sends out gospel laborers into his abundant harvest field (Matt. 9:37–38). Prayer humbles our hearts, shapes our desires, spurs our obedience, and invokes the mercy of a God who delights to save sinners. For the work of evangelism, we have no better tool.

In the 1950s, a man named Ekaso served as a church elder in Wolaitta, Ethiopia. He was present at an annual church convention when Mahae, an evangelist, stood and pleaded for gospel workers to go to several tribes in Ethiopia's Omo River Valley. Mahae asked the assembled believers to pray for God to send six men. Missionary Dick McLellan reports:

> As Mahae sat down, Ekaso jumped up. . . . He led in a fervent prayer for the Lord to send six new evangelists with Mahae to the Omo Valley. As we said, "Amen," Ekaso challenged men to go. Five men came forward and said they would go! Ekaso asked, "Is there one more? Who will go?" Everyone was silent. There was no response. Then Ekaso answered his own appeal! "Then I will go!" he said.[8]

For many years after that day, Ekaso labored as an evangelist; God used him to plant several churches, first in the Omo Valley and then in other parts of Ethiopia.

Like Ekaso's prayer, the prayer of every evangelist is an act of dependence on God. We know that one may plant gospel seed and another may faithfully sprinkle gospel water, but God is the one who makes soul seedlings grow (1 Cor. 3:6–7). On our knees, we acknowledge our own weakness and ask the sovereign God to work in our hearts and the hearts of our neighbors. In prayer too, we submit our desires to God[9] and train ourselves to want the things he wants. When we pray faithfully for our neighbors to come to Christ and be saved, our naturally indifferent hearts are continually stirred with compassion for their souls.

And a regular habit of prayer moves us to action. Like Ekaso, we find ourselves rising from our knees to take up the work ourselves. When the members of the early church were threatened by intense persecution, they "lifted their voices together to God" praying, "Grant to your servants to continue to speak your word with all boldness." And then, "when they had prayed, the place in which they were gathered together was shaken, and they were all filled with the Holy Spirit and continued to speak the word of God with boldness" (Acts 4:24, 29, 31). As we pray, we may discover that God's answer to our request for bold evangelists is *us*.

Horatius Bonar wrote in his *Words to Winners of Souls*: "We are weak in the pulpit because we are weak in the closet."[10] Do you desire greater confidence in proclaiming the gospel to your neighbors? Then pray. Pray in private. Pray with your family. Pray with your community. Pray with the gathered church. Pray for God's name to be hallowed. Pray for his kingdom to advance. Pray for widespread obedience to his will. At all times and without ceasing, pray. And then look eagerly for God's gracious answer.

HOLINESS

The next resource needed by those who tell the good news is a life of personal holiness. The Bible exhorts every believer: "As he who called you is holy, you also be holy in all your conduct" (1 Pet. 1:15). A life of obedience to God's commands is not optional for the person who has been ransomed, adopted, and set apart by God. Each of us must increasingly—and by the indispensable help of the Holy Spirit—hate sin and love God's law. We will never do this perfectly, but we must do it diligently, echoing the familiar prayer of Robert Murray M'Cheyne: "Lord, make me as holy as a pardoned sinner can be."[11]

This life of holiness is an important part of evangelism. I once heard a pastor recount a conversation he had at a conference where he was preaching. After the service, an elderly man had approached the pastor to thank him for the sermon. As they talked, the man revealed that he had only recently been converted. The pastor was intrigued and asked the old man what had been the instrument to bring him to faith. The man replied, "The faithful testimony of my godly parents." Though dead, his parents still spoke. Their lives of obedience to Christ resounded through the decades, ringing in their son's ears and calling him to faith.

What an encouragement this is to Christian parents and to all who sincerely practice obedience to God! Our daily acts of obedience can be used by the Lord to awaken faith in our neighbors. As your car pulls out of the driveway every Sunday morning on its way to church, you reinforce the existence of an unseen God to your watching neighbors. As you speak kindly to your children on the playground, you demonstrate the Spirit's power to listening ears all around you. As you refuse to participate in office gossip, you bring honor to Christ in the break room. Even in your response to your own sin—admitting wrong and asking forgiveness—you testify to the truth of the gospel you proclaim.

Sadly, the opposite is also true. If we are unkind to those around us, if we dismiss the needs of others and speak harshly to our family members, if we are more often at the ballpark than at church on Sunday, if we ignore our sin and fail to repent, we communicate to our neighbors that God is not important and his Spirit is impotent. As Al Mohler explains, "We shouldn't expect that the gospel will have credibility if we don't look like gospel people."[12]

The Bible commands us to "be blameless and innocent, children of God without blemish in the midst of a crooked and twisted generation, among whom you shine as lights in the world" (Phil. 2:15). We pursue holiness because we live before the face of God, and also because we live in view of our neighbors. Are we telling our neighbors to repent and turn from their sin? Then we must show them by our lives that repentance and new obedience are possible with the Spirit. Are we calling our neighbors to submit themselves to the will of God? Then we must joyfully submit ourselves. Are we pleading with our neighbors to call out to God in prayer and to find him as he is revealed in the Bible? Then we must be people who diligently practice those means of grace. As the great evangelist Charles Spurgeon asserted, "A man who is to be a soul winner must have holiness of character."[13]

COMMITMENT TO THE LOCAL CHURCH

Jim is a man in our church who was an unbeliever well into adulthood. While he was serving time in prison, a chaplain ministered to him and pressed him with the gospel, and—by the power of the Spirit—Jim came to Christ. For a few years, he served his remaining prison sentence as a believer, studying the Word of God and growing in knowledge of Christ. After his release, the chaplain directed him to our church. For Jim, the experience of church life is entirely new. He did not grow up in the church, and even his first years as a believer were spent apart from the church as he was confined to prison. But over the past few months, he has participated in public worship, eaten meals with church members, joined in prayer meetings and book studies, and involved himself in the whole life of the church. On a recent Sunday, Jim gave testimony to how being welcomed into our church had radically changed his life. He finished by saying simply, "I never had a people before."

The fact that you have "a people" may be something that, after years in the church, you rarely marvel about anymore. But God's delight in his gathered church is unflagging. It is "the church of God, which he obtained with his own blood" (Acts 20:28). The church is where Christ's fullness dwells and where God's manifold wisdom is revealed (Eph. 3:10; 4:11–16). The gospel and the church are inseparable—Christ died and was raised again, not merely to secure the salvation of individuals but to ransom a people for himself. As Hughes Oliphant Old explains, the Christian life comes with the directive, "Assembly required."[14]

Commitment to the local church is also one of your vital resources as an evangelist. In the church, you are yourself discipled. You join with God's people to receive his Word, offer him worship, use your gifts for his glory, and serve his saints. Two skills that you most need—handling God's Word rightly and talking easily about it with others—are modeled, encouraged, and practiced in the church.

Moreover, to invite someone to church is to invite them to hear the gospel proclaimed with power and to see the gospel lived out in the lives of a diverse group of people. In the last section, we discussed the importance of a life of holiness for effective evangelism, and we should note that such holiness cannot be practiced in solitude. Many of the Lord's commands are commands for the gathered church. *Be kind*, says the Lord. *Forgive. Give to those in need. Bear one another's burdens. Encourage one another. Exhort one another. Pray for one another. Practice hospitality.* This mutual love testifies to Christ. Jesus said, "By this all people will know that you are my disciples, if you have love for one another" (John 13:35), and the church father Tertullian famously pictured pagans observing the Christians around them with amazement, saying, "Look how they love one another!" As we obey God's commands in the context of the church, we bear witness to the power of the Spirit to transform all kinds of people into a holy community—and we invite our neighbors to join us.

We have seen, then, how the whole life of faith equips and compels evangelism. When our hearts are delighted by Christ, when we are faithful in prayer and dedicated to holiness, when we join ourselves to the local church, we will be ready (and eager!) to assist our spiritually needy neighbors. These things are not particularly flashy, and they certainly are not new. And yet they are the spiritual supply that God gives to equip evangelists for their spiritual task. Horatius Bonar wrote, "What a mystery! The soul and eternity of one man depends upon the voice of another!"[15] Oh, that we would cultivate our hearts so our voices will ring out, strongly and clearly telling our neighbors the way to be saved!

The Cultural Mandate and the Great Commission

Camille Hallstrom

Introduction by Kathleen Nielson

INTRODUCTION

When God created the first male and female in his own image, he called them to "be fruitful and multiply and fill the earth and subdue it and have dominion over the fish of the sea and over the birds of the heavens and over every living thing that moves on the earth" (Gen. 1:27–28). To these human beings God gave dominion over all the rest of creation. When Adam and Eve worked and kept the garden (2:15), they were exercising that God-given dominion.

When farmers today grow crops, or when chemists discover drugs that prevent or cure diseases, they are exercising God-given dominion. When artists create scenes in oil paints, or shape stories in words . . . when a housekeeper cleans a bathroom, or a cook creates a dinner . . . all these activities are exercising dominion over creation. Whether we are aware of it or not, according to God's Word, all of us human creators are reflecting the image of our Creator God—shaping creation after him.

This "cultural mandate," as we call it, still stands: we human beings were made to reflect the image of our Creator in filling and ruling the earth. As we raise families, create cultures and civilizations, and labor to sustain and grow them, we are following God's mandate from creation. Faithfully following that mandate glorifies the God who made us.

But how does this mandate from creation relate to the Bible's whole story of the fall, redemption, and the promised restoration of all things in Christ? Ever since the first human beings sinned, fallen human beings have not been able faithfully to fulfill that creation mandate; the image of God in us is tainted, dimmed. How can we sinful women and men bring glory to our Creator?

The cultural mandate is incomplete without the good news of the gospel. I might be able to create the most compelling art or figure out how to grow the highest-yield crops or raise the most disciplined and productive children, but without having my sins covered by the blood of Christ, after this short life I will face eternity without my Creator and under his wrath. I, as a believer, might teach a nonbeliever to write or sing or clean floors with excellence; I might save his life through landmark medical discoveries. But if he does not hear and believe the gospel, he has been only temporarily helped.

The good news of the gospel, however, lets the creation mandate shine, as by faith human beings are forgiven of their sin and restored into the image of Christ their Redeemer—who is himself the image of God. In Christ, God's mandate from creation is and will be completely fulfilled through his redeemed people on this earth that he created for them to fill and rule. On this side of the cross, the cultural mandate and the Great Commission merge, to the end of seeing the earth filled with the knowledge of the glory of the Lord Jesus.

Gloria and I are delighted that Camille Hallstrom, professor of theatre, is willing to share some stories and some musings from her context: How do the cultural mandate and the Great Commission go together? It's a question God's people must all consider as we travel the diverse pathways through which he calls us to exercise dominion over his creation, all for the glory of Christ the Lord.

———

CHRISTIANS AND ART

I am the founder and chair of the theatre department at Covenant College, a small Christian liberal arts school in Lookout Mountain, Georgia. Prior to that, for ten years, I taught in the theatre department of a nearby state university. During my time there I sent out prayer letters asking people to pray for me as though I were a missionary in the field—which, of course, I was. I needed prayer to be a good witness of Jesus Christ via the quality of my work and collegiality; to be salt and light in an environment that often unwittingly promoted social and personal decay; and to point the way of deliverance, salvation, and hope to people whose very work often could be a personal degradation. An excerpt from one such letter follows:

> Earlier this fall we produced an evening of one-act plays by prominent women playwrights. . . . If I had been aware of the content of the one play before it started rehearsal, I would have objected to its being done. Not only were the verbal assault and sexual violence of the play an affront to the audience (I heard people around me *groaning*), but the student-actors who were called upon to enact such things have, in my opinion, been betrayed by a faculty (I include myself) which should have known better than to proffer such caustic lye as a profitable exercise for students to immerse themselves in. Please pray for the fallout of this event in the department. . . . [1]

To the degree that Christians think about the theatre and film worlds at all, I'm afraid it is often only to complain about the ungodliness of both the stories and the artists bringing those stories to life. To be sure, as the letter above demonstrates, dramatic art in our culture has often been used by the Enemy to model ungodly attitudes and behaviors, and since "bad company ruins good morals" (1 Cor. 15:33), we must continually pray for wisdom concerning what we watch—and what we in the theatre portray. But as H. R. Rookmaaker once wrote in his sobering *Modern Art and the Death of a Culture*:

> This art is the work of your neighbors, your contemporaries, human beings who are crying out in despair for the loss of their humanity, their values, their lost absolutes, groping in the dark for answers. . . . If we want to help our generation we must hear their cry. We must listen to them as they cry out from their prison, the prison of a universe which is aimless, meaningless, absurd.[2]

"It is our prayer that students here are prepared to become 'missionaries' to the dramatic professions," reads Covenant College's theatre webpage. "We seek to help them become both skilled in dramatic craft and mature in Christian discipleship, that they might one day enter the professional stage and film worlds in order to produce fine art to the glory of God, but also to reach out to a lost 'people group' [dramatic professionals] who will not very likely be reached by outsiders."

We also want our graduates to grow skills for reaching contemporary audiences. Francis Schaeffer once stipulated a proper "order for . . . apologetics in the second half of the twentieth century [i.e.,] knowledge precedes faith."[3] Today's twenty-first-century realities require us to update that order. If knowledge preceded faith for the modern person, perhaps *intuition* of knowledge must precede knowledge for the cynical-about-truth, postmodern person. Hilary

Brand and Adrienne Chaplin describe our twenty-first-century situation this way:

> We can no longer believe in any truth claims that declare themselves to be the key to understanding the whole of life. Whether they are the meta-narratives (grand stories) of Marx or Freud . . . Christianity, or the Enlightenment, they are no longer credible. . . . In an age when bald statements of capital-T Truth are discounted, society turns to its poets and artists for the most truthful accounts of the human condition. "Grand Stories" may be treated with the utmost suspicion, but people will listen to any number of stories on a human scale, especially those that come from the depths of experience.[4]

While any given story "on a human scale" cannot subsume the entirety of the biblical *creation-fall-redemption-restoration* metanarrative, nevertheless such stories can reflect that metanarrative in various ways. A tale of deep human suffering points to the reality of the fall; a character grappling with guilt exposes our need for forgiveness; a plot in which one person's self-sacrifice is the means to save another illustrates the nature of redemption. The telling of such tales is not (and indeed, shouldn't be expected to be) a substitute for evangelism. Art, by and large, does not serve well as evangelism *per se*; rather, its great strength is as *pre*-evangelism. When a skilled artist, created in the image of the Creator God, shapes stories that truthfully reflect reality—whether or not that artist is even aware of the God he images—such work can touch the depths of human longing and need. Only Jesus Christ, of course, can fill those depths, nevertheless God is quite able to use such stories (and art in general) to awaken people to their need of a Savior.

I once wrote a poem based on Old Testament imagery. Sometime later, while teaching acting at the state university, I included my poem with the other texts we were performing. The students were rapt. "*Where* did you get this from?" asked one—a young man who was homosexual and HIV positive. I told them I had written it drawing on passages in which God speaks to Israel as his adulterous bride, and we then proceeded to work on it as we would any other text. Some years later, another student from that class contacted me specifically to ask for a copy of the poem: "I've lost mine, and need it." In conversations with that young man, it seemed to me that the message of the Scriptures had somehow touched his heart. I do not know whether he might ever have become a Christian, nevertheless he once said to me, "I have no patience with all those university types who malign Christianity. Do they know what they're talking about? It's such a *beautiful* religion!"

The people around us today will not be easily evangelized with a propositional tract; we must gain entry by another door. Move a person's heart by an encounter with real beauty and he may just end by asking, "*Where* did you get this from?"[5] It is for just this reason that I write director's notes for the programs of plays I direct. Often we schedule discussion forums after performances as well. In the context of beauty shared in human relationship can come opportunity to share biblical truth with one who needs to hear. And then that truth will set him free.[6]

CASE STUDY: *WIT* AND WAODANI

"Theatre," we say at Covenant College, "is incarnation." Not only is the *end* of theatrical production incarnational (inasmuch as actors "enflesh" the words of a text), we also must make the *means* of production incarnational. That is, the theatre—as a *collaborative art form*, shared as a *collective experience* with audiences—is involved at every turn with *human relationships*. Thus, in our production practices—i.e., how we behave with each other onstage and backstage, our consideration of the impact our play selections will have on those who see them, and how we handle business dealings with theatre professionals—we must "incarnate

Christ" for everyone we encounter. In other words, we must keep the call to love one another foremost in our theory, planning, and prayers.

Christians wishing to work in the dramatic arts must, for example, learn integrity in their business practices. Many might think nothing of editing a play in which they found objectionable material. But carving up a playwright's work not only does not constitute treating my neighbor as I would be treated; it is a violation of contractual obligations. If it's necessary to secure rights to perform a play, and I cannot abide by the agreement to present the text "without any changes, additions, alterations or deletions,"[7] I must, for love's sake, forgo producing that particular play.

In 2004, I had occasion to correspond on such a matter with Margaret Edson, author of the 1999 Pulitzer Prize–winning drama *Wit*. *Wit*'s story follows Vivian Bearing, a scholar of John Donne's *Holy Sonnets*, who is dying of ovarian cancer. An uncompromising and impersonal scholar, Vivian gains painful self-awareness through the indignities she suffers at the hands of her equally uncompromising and impersonal student doctor, Jason Posner. In one particularly gut-wrenching scene, Jason performs a brusque, impatient pelvic exam on Vivian. The exam ends abruptly with a loudly uttered expletive, as a startled but unapologetic Jason feels just how huge Vivian's tumor is.

The play's final image, the staging of Vivian's death, reflects an earlier commentary on "Sonnet 10": "Nothing but a breath, a comma, separates life from life everlasting."[8] Thus—almost anticlimactically, following the pandemonium of staff attempts to shock her back to life—Vivian quietly rises from her bed, removes her ID bracelet and gown, and, standing naked in a pool of heaven's light, reaches skyward. Lights down. Play over.

> "Very simple, really. . . . death is no longer something to act out on a stage, with exclamation points. It's a comma, a pause."[9]

I was understandably eager to produce *Wit* with my college students. But the play's final nude image, together with some occasional language usage, rendered doing so problematic.

So what to do?

Do unto others as I'd have them do unto me: have the courage to contact the playwright, asking permission to bowdlerize her script.

Oh, dear.

Of course, I assumed she'd dismiss me as a fundamentalist crackpot, ball up my letter, and throw it away. Still, I wrote, praying continually as I did. I asked God not only for this Pulitzer winner to grant my requested alterations, but that she might somehow find what I had to write oddly refreshing. When I summoned the courage to finally drop the letter in the mail, I tacked on a last-minute, it-couldn't-happen, yet-nothing-is-impossible-with-God prayer: "Oh, and while you're at it, Father, do you think you could bring her to campus to discuss the play?"

In the following, the reader will see referenced a number of factors I think through when selecting a play for production: literary quality, philosophic weight, suitability for the given audience and particular cast and crew. Hopefully the letter also demonstrates attempts, as mentioned above, to love—to incarnate Christ for—my audience, my actors, and a theatre professional in the wider world.

> Dear Ms. Edson,
>
> . . . For several years I have wanted to produce your remarkable play *Wit* here at Covenant College. For so many reasons it is a play that ought to be produced and seen by the sort of faculty and students we tend to attract . . . [not least because] our Presbyterian culture can sometimes . . . produce minds-count-more-than-matter scholars. [Thus] a play which treats similar characters via Vivian Bearing and Jason Posner might be a dose of much-needed medicine. Our folk should hear [character] Professor Ashford's exhortation that, in addi-

tion to scholarly rigor, sometimes the pursuit of truth requires that we "Don't go back to the library. Go out. Enjoy yourself with friends. Hmm?"

After struggling for some while with casting difficulties, finally it is my hope to produce *Wit* in February 2005. But before I can do so, I must first ask you an unusual favor. As part of the integration of my discipline and faith, I impress on my student actors the necessity to take seriously the language and actions they employ onstage. It seems to me that the influence enactments have on actors' and audiences' hearts and minds is underestimated in the broader theatre education community. What we do onstage really isn't all "just pretend." It isn't reasonable, for example, to expect two actors to walk away from a scene of physical intimacy unchanged. (Indeed, the casting problem I referenced above has to do with this very point. As a teacher, I must guard the tender hearts of my students. How does one ask two teenaged actors to perform a pelvic exam onstage? Enormously dramatically important and compassion-evoking, there is no conscionable way to alter the scene. Nevertheless, there is no conscionable way for me to require my young charges to bring it to life in public. Problem solved however, as two of my most capable students were recently married, and when presented with the opportunity to play Vivian and Jason, they jumped at the chance. Hurrah!)[10]

. . . It will come as no surprise that in producing plays at a Christian undergraduate institution, we pay close attention to such things as language usage and nudity. I would like to stage the final moment of the play when Vivian passes from death to life with my actress wearing, perhaps, a white satin slip, small enough to have been hidden under her hospital gowns during the show. Also, I am requesting your permission to alter some few instances of language. . . . I am aware that it is no minor matter to ask a writer for permission to alter her wording. I feel presumptuous, yet in my situation it is a choice between making such alterations or not producing the play at all. I hope so very much that you will give me your permission, since I want so very much to do your play. . . .

I thank you for your time and consideration, and look eagerly for your reply.

With warm regards,
Camille Hallstrom

Edson's reply:

Dear Ms. Hallstrom,

Thank you for writing to me about *Wit*. Of course I am thoroughly opposed to change of one syllable; of course, how would I ever know if you went ahead and did it anyway? You were sweet and honorable to ask, so yes, I give my permission and blessing.

I am interested in you and your work. Got some good grades, did ya? Summa slamma jamma; good for you! (I looked you up.) Theater and religion go so well and so awkwardly together. I'm curious how they're coming together for you and your students.

I have done a lot of speaking in conjunction with the play. I am asking you to invite me to Covenant to speak when you produce *Wit*. To me *Wit* is a hugely Christian play, yet I am rarely asked about that. I'm eager for the chance to talk—and listen—in a hugely Christian context.

Inviting me will cause some trouble. (Look me up!) Your superiors will probably say no. In that case, let's meet halfway for a cup of coffee, just us two.

Very truly yours,
Maggie Edson

She said, "Yes!"; she said, "YES!" And more than that, she *asked me* if she could come to campus! Wow! This prayer stuff works!

Still, she was right; my superiors did have some hesitation about her coming. For, in "looking her up," I discovered she identified herself as gay and was living in a long-term relationship with another woman and their two little boys. Some discussion followed with the administration about how best to handle the situation: How might we bring this exceptional literary light to campus for all to benefit by without potentially stirring up a hornet's nest, or miscommunicating about an important topic? For her part, Ms. Edson graciously volunteered that, though others might make an issue of her personal life, she had no intention of even mentioning it. She only wanted to talk about, and listen to us talk about, the *play*. Thus, in the months before her visit, I and the cast and crew prayed that God would help us show her genuine hospitality, and that he would keep her and us safe from needless, public contention.

What eventually ensued was a witty, erudite, and enthusiastically well-received public presentation by Ms. Edson. Stemming from that experience has been an ongoing relationship. Since she lives nearby, I will, sometimes with a church pal or students in tow, travel to Atlanta to see a play and then meet up for coffee. "Maggie" has written me an academic reference, she is on the mailing list for prayer letters about my mission work in Uganda and South Sudan, and she has thanked me for making her aware of realities abroad she might not otherwise have known. When asked whether she'd object to my writing about this history, she gave her enthusiastic approval.

A year after getting to know Maggie Edson, I shared the story with a production company I thought might need the encouragement. Every Tribe Entertainment (ETE) had planned to produce a film, *End of the Spear*, in time for the fiftieth anniversary of the deaths of five missionaries (Jim Elliot, Nate Saint, et al.) who were murdered in their attempted outreach to the Waodani people in Ecuador. After signing a fine actor, Chad Allen, to play both Nate Saint and his son Steve, ETE discovered Allen was a vocal gay activist. The producers and the families of the martyrs—particularly

Steve Saint, who served as a go-between for the company, the Waodani, and the families—were shocked. But they decided, after much prayer, that God would have them abide by their contract with Allen, even though his own life was so at odds with biblical teaching and with the legacy of the men he played.[11] Many Christians condemned, sometimes quite viciously, the film's producer Mart Green, and even Saint himself, for keeping Allen in the role.[12] Allen, for his part, was able to make the following statement concerning his experience working on the film with these men:

> I was anxious to meet Steve and when I did, in the most perfect sense, Steve was the realest person I'd met. . . . He cried in our first meeting over dinner, I cried. . . . I remember writing [in my journal], at the end of the day . . . "if nothing else comes of this movie . . . that's the kind of man I want to be."[13]

In an email to ETE, having mentioned my vision to train Christians to become missionaries to the professional stage and film worlds, I thanked ETE for providing my students with such a valuable model:

> I praise God for this entire situation! In addition to having a good film to share with my students, I have something even more important: an example of Christian production folk dealing in integrity with a representative of a community who has every reason to view Christians with suspicion and hostility.
>
> Just as the five missionaries and their families had to risk so much to bring the gospel to the Waodani, Christian dramatists are going to have to risk much to bring Christ to the broken, hurting, needy folk who populate the profession. Who could have foretold that God would use the very men who killed those missionaries to later travel the globe to bring inspiration and God's comfort to countless thousands? Likewise, who knows what God has in mind for the Chad Allens of the world? But be sure that by your demonstrating Christian love and professional integrity to [Chad] when so many were criticizing, even

slandering, you will bring a great harvest one day. I am eager to see what story God is currently crafting as he intertwines the lives of Every Tribe Entertainment, the Saints, and Chad Allen. Maybe one day another movie will be made about that!

A TIME TO SPEAK

For every kind of missionary, there is—and there must be—a time to speak the Bible's truth of Jesus who died on the cross to save sinners, who rose from the dead, and who lives even now, empowering believers through his Holy Spirit. Sometimes that time to speak comes with years of relationship, friendship, and integrity (and sometimes the conversation goes on for years). Sometimes it comes in a fleeting moment, perhaps in a question about the reason for our hope—a question we must be prepared to answer with gentleness and respect (1 Pet. 3:15–16). It comes with prayer. It often comes through bringing friends into the fellowship of believers where the Word of God is taught and lived; no believer spreads the light alone.

But how important to embed all these moments in lives of salt and light that honor God by pointing toward truth in every possible, beautiful way.

4

Mercy Ministry and Proclamation Ministry

Putting Them Together

Eowyn Stoddard

EVANGELISM: A TWO-SIDED COIN

In this chapter, we will be looking at how God's Word proclaimed and his mercy applied to human need are bound inextricably in God's nature and his great mission of redemption in Christ. Word and deed are the two sides of the evangelism coin.[1] Jesus calls his bride, the church, to serve him in carrying out his mission to purchase back his destitute people. She is to be remade in his image, learn to deal in his currency, and trust in his economy until the day he restores all things.

Sharon's Story

Sharon, a medical doctor who serves on the mission field, tells the following story:

The national church in a sensitive country invited us to help reach a rural area in the hills by providing free medical care. The local authorities restricted our access but allowed us to treat patients in a nearby town. Patients came in great numbers, including a few from the hills. With the assistance of local believers, each person received medical care, a listening ear, and, if so desired, prayer. After we left, national believers followed up with them and began a Bible study. The following year, I recognized a frail, elderly man with Coke-bottle glasses. He grabbed my hand and excitedly told me of a busload of new patients coming from his village. He was one of the new believers from the hills! By our third visit, we traveled up to the hills. It was Sunday. About halfway up, we rounded a bend and, arrayed before us was a multitude of smiling people of all ages reaching out to greet us. Mats were spread outside a little brick and tin church, already too small for the growing congregation. Some of our former patients were among the first members! How we enjoyed the songs of praise, the prayers, and breaking bread together that morning! What a gift to have been a small part of God's plan to capture the hearts of these precious brothers and sisters and to enlarge the family of faith!

Question: Which was most important in this story, the ministry of mercy or the proclamation of the Word? This beautiful story of redemption showcases how God accomplished the salvation of his elect people through his saving truth delivered in mercy, resulting in a new body of believers.[2] But how does this work? Word and deed are two sides of the coin—but is it a coin to be flipped indiscriminately? Truth and mercy are bound together—but how?

GOD'S INVESTMENT PLAN

From the beginning, God had a plan to invest himself in his creation so people could know him intimately, love, and worship him. He did it through creating Adam and Eve in his image, appointing them as managers over his ecosystem and providing for all their physical, relational, and spiritual needs.[3] Regretfully, this wasn't enough for our first parents, and they squandered their God-given investment. Since then, every aspect of our life in this fallen world is affected by spiritual bankruptcy. Sin destroyed the spiritual communion of human beings with their Creator; this ultimate need unmet results in brokenness and need on every other level.

But God responded to Adam and Eve's need for a savior through *truthful words* and *merciful actions*. Clearly the categories overlap, but we can see that he ensured their physical protection by making for them clothing of animal skins. He responded with relational provision, confirming their marriage relationship and giving them offspring. His physical and relational provision point to his ultimate provision: God intervened spiritually. Though Adam and Eve's failure had severe consequences for them and the rest of humanity, he gave them a promise of a seed who would someday defeat Satan, sin, and death, and reverse the effects of the disaster they had caused.

Here we see God's currency of truth and mercy, deposited in seed form. Subsequently, the gradual revelation of God's plan of redemption in the Old Testament broadened in scope but not in nature. It included a trifold promise to match our trifold need: physical real estate, a new community reflective of God's mercy, and that which makes all the rest possible—the presence of God with his people. From garden, to tent, to temple, to human flesh, God had always planned to meet his people's needs in person. He simply revealed it gradually until he did it perfectly in his own Son.

In the days of Christ's life on earth, the godlike image of the ruling emperor was minted on coins. The ubiquitous denarii symbolized the reach of his power throughout the empire.[4] In the same way, the King of the universe invested all his divine assets into Jesus, his beloved Son and treasured possession. The second Adam successfully reflected God's image: "He is the image of the invisible God" (Col. 1:15), "a man who was a prophet mighty in *deed* and *word* before God and all the people" (Luke 24:19). Jesus Christ embodied and unified the two sides of God's purchasing power in his person: the mighty Word of God and his merciful deeds—he is the Word made flesh. Jesus was not just a prophet. He was God in the flesh and would pay the ultimate price with his life to unleash God's redemptive power to the ends of the earth (Phil. 2:5–8).

TOKENS OF THE COVENANT

Jesus's modus operandi during his earthly ministry was a union of word and mercy (Matt. 9:35–10:1). Though there is again overlap in the categories, his word-based ministry included calling his disciples, teaching in formal and informal settings, preaching, storytelling, encouraging, rebuking, praying, and forgiving sins. His mercy-based ministry included healing, feeding crowds, exorcisms, resuscitations, miracles over nature, showing compassion to the poor, and defending social outcasts. His miracles perfectly combined word and mercy, not for two different ends but for one: they brought physical good as signs of spiritual good in order to call people to faith. We might think of his deeds of mercy as "tokens" of the saving truth he came to reveal. Consider these three examples:

Token 1: Come Buy without Money

Jesus was moved by compassion when he saw his people hungry and without a shepherd. After feeding five thousand men, he asserted: "I am the bread of life; whoever comes to me shall not hunger, and whoever believes in me shall never thirst" (John 6:35). This miracle reminded the Jewish crowd of the provision of manna in the desert. Jesus used a basic human need to point people to their ultimate need for eternal life in him. The words on this token read: *This free bread and water are a sign to you of*

God's gracious provision of Christ, the true source of your life and sustenance (see Isa. 55:1).

Token 2: Is Health the Greatest Wealth?

Jesus had tender compassion on people whose physical ailments hindered their ability to work or worship in community. Though he often healed, he clearly established a priority of spiritual over physical healing: "For which is easier, to say, 'Your sins are forgiven,' or to say, 'Rise and walk'?" (Matt. 9:5) Healings meant more than just the temporary relief of physical suffering. They were eschatological intrusions pointing to Jesus's divinity and power to initiate the great reversal when all suffering and decay will finally cease. The people Jesus healed on earth still died in the end. It was their spiritual healing that ensured they would live eternally with resurrected bodies in glory. This token bears the engraving: *I, the Son of God, have the power to heal and restore you because I have vanquished sin and its devastating side effects. Trust me with the healing of your soul and the rest will come!*[5]

Token 3: Best Wine

An interesting token miracle is Jesus's first: he turned water into wine at a wedding (John 2:1–11). It seems strange to think of wine as a *need* that Jesus was meeting, but the miracle points to a deeper reality. Throughout the Old Testament, wine was a symbol of the covenant blessing for Israel. Moreover, the bridegroom at a wedding was supposed to provide the best wine for his guests. Jesus announced without a word that he was *the* Bridegroom, equating himself with Yahweh (see Isa. 54:5; Jer. 3:6–14)[6] and providing blessing for Israel through his perfect obedience. The message from God on this token reads: *You need a relationship with the Bridegroom, who provides all covenant blessings freely!*

These tokens were validations of Jesus's identity and mission as well as signs pointing forward to his sacrifice on the cross.[7] There, he experienced all three areas of need on our behalf. The Bread of Life was hungry, and the living water cried, "I thirst" (John 19:28). The friend of sinners suffered betrayal and was wounded for our transgressions (Isa. 53:5). The perfect Israelite cried out, "My God, why have you forsaken me?" (Matt. 27:46) experiencing the ultimate agony: spiritual alienation from his heavenly Father. God's greatest proclamation of truth and greatest act of mercy converge at the cross. The gospel is the good news that God forgives sins through the work of Christ who died in our place and rose again, and this gospel has cosmic implications: all things will be renewed *in him* (Rom. 8:20–22; Col. 1:20). God confirmed Christ's work with the stamp of approval of the resurrection. The bride of Christ was bought not by silver or gold, but by the precious and powerful blood of Jesus that ransomed us from sin and death—and that redeems a people who will live as Christ's body in restored bodies in a new creation forever. Having experienced the efficacy of his redemption, we cannot divorce what Jesus held together perfectly; we must, like him, love in word and in deed.

AMBASSADORS

Bridal Shower

As the redeemed bride of Christ, the church shares the same mission as her Bridegroom. This task may sound daunting, but God in his mercy showered the early church with the Holy Spirit at Pentecost and empowered her to become the *ezer*[8] of Christ, perfectly fitted to do his work by the help of the Paraclete. She is his gifted ambassador, sent on his mission to represent his kingdom truth and merciful rule to the ends of the earth. "We are ambassadors for Christ, God making his appeal through us. We *implore you* on behalf of Christ, be reconciled to God" (2 Cor. 5:20). As ambassadors, we are called to spread his rule as we deal in his currency—imploring through word and deed.

Expense Account

In Jesus's day, ambassadors of the Greco-Roman world received expense money called the *ephodia* to travel, establish embassies, and set up the culture of the emperor in his stead.[9] As ambassadors of Christ, we are disbursed as an *ephodia* to accomplish the task of the Great Commission. It is the treasure chest of spiritual gifts that equips us for spreading the gospel. Peter's simple categorization of the spiritual gifts given to the church for mission is twofold:[10]

> Each one should use whatever gift he has received to serve others, faithfully administering God's grace in its various forms. If anyone *speaks*,[11] he should do it as one speaking the very words of God. If anyone *serves*,[12] he should do it with the strength God provides, so that in all things God may be praised through Jesus Christ. (1 Pet. 4:10–11; see also Rom. 12:6–8; 1 Cor. 12:4–11; 12:28)

Peter's logic here is that there are two distinct yet inseparable types of gifts, speaking and serving, and that both are needed for God's grace to be administered effectively. The body as a whole has the necessary gifts for mission. This does not mean, however, that certain members of the body exclusively speak and some only ever serve in practical ways. Such an understanding could lead either to a lack of willing, humble service or to fearful silence. We all need to be challenged in our areas of weakness while appreciating the strengths of others in the body.

And we all need to base our lives and all our service on the truth given in God's Word: by that Word we have been made wise for salvation and have been fed with the Bread of Life. It is the Word that commands us to serve as a means of proving the truth of the message. Therefore both word and deed are important, and they are important together. But one is primary in the sense that it is the prerequisite for ultimate well being: without God's Word, which has the power to effect spiritual change, we have no life, and no real life to give. "For what does it profit a man to gain the whole world and forfeit his life?" (Mark 8:36).

Putting Our Money Where Our Mouth Is

On the one hand, speaking is meeting a spiritual need. It could be tempting to say that the one who speaks isn't *doing* anything. However, there is true power in the Word when it is preached, spoken in counseling, or used to encourage or witness. God's Word has the last word when it comes to addressing our physical, relational, and spiritual needs (2 Tim. 3:16; 2 Pet. 1:3). We are to speak the very words of God, not our own. God's Spirit-breathed Word alone has the power to convict of sin, create new life, and renovate the heart.

Serving, on the other hand, is speaking to practical needs. And just as speaking has active spiritual power, so also has serving, as God uses it for eternal good. Peter points to the example of believing wives married to unbelieving husbands outside the church. A wife's loving sacrifice, not preachy prose, has the power to woo her husband to Christ and prepare his heart to be receptive to the words of the gospel (1 Pet. 3:1–2). One of the refugees in a recent baptismal class shared:

> My wife had changed so much while we were still in our home country! She used to worry a lot, and now she was peaceful and served joyfully! I knew something supernatural was happening with her, so I asked her about it and she said she had met Jesus. She invited me to go with her to an underground house church, but in the end, we had to flee. God had a plan to bring me to Germany so I could find Jesus. Through reading the Bible, he showed me Jesus was the only way to God. Now I want to live my life for Jesus, body, heart, mind, and soul.

In his divine economy, God uses the church's witness of word and deed to bless the world. It is therefore no surprise that the same twofold categorization of the gifts is reflected in the leadership structure of the church body.[13] A biblical model of church includes both elders and deacons—servants of the Word and servants of mercy—coordinated to serve its members and advance the gospel. Many parachurch organizations or NGOs do a lot of good and strategic work for God's kingdom, but a full-orbed *gospel ministry* must centrally involve the church. In turn, the church must address people's physical, relational, and spiritual needs in word and in deed if she wants to see life-changing evangelism, discipleship, and church planting take place. The church's main ambassadorial calling focuses on word and mercy that bear fruit for the kingdom and not simply on humanitarian activism. Despite all her flaws, the church is at the center of God's economy of redemption.

MAXIMIZING INVESTMENTS

Where to Start?

Years ago, a friend invited me to be at the birth of her second child. She showed me some Bible verses on notecards she had prepared for herself to help cope with labor. As contractions intensified, her husband reached for a card and read a verse. Can you guess her response? She couldn't hear the truth of the verse through the pain. She simply needed her husband to help her concentrate on her breathing. Similarly, we must differentiate between "presenting needs" and "ultimate needs" when we do evangelism. "Mission may not always *begin* with evangelism. But mission that does not ultimately *include* declaring the Word and the name of Christ, the call to repentance, and faith and obedience has not completed its task. It is defective mission, not holistic mission."[14]

Where to start in evangelism is not always obvious. Thomas Manton wrote, "The more affected we are with our misery, the fitter for Christ's mercy."[15] For the first time in our own family's short personal history of missions in Germany, we are seeing displaced people asking about how they can know and follow Jesus. Their losses and disillusionment with Islam in particular have prepared their hearts for the gospel in unexpected ways. It is much easier for us to point people to Christ when they are aware of their need—a lot harder, however, when affluence deceives with the illusion of autonomy and safety.

Prosperity can be the greatest enemy of the gospel. Colleagues working in an opulent part of Germany describe the people there as "materially wealthy but spiritually destitute." Christians in American suburbia share a similar challenge. It takes a lot of time listening to friends and neighbors to discern how they are hurting and how the gospel intersects with their greatest needs. Often their need is relational. Marriage, parenting, or other interpersonal issues can be excellent avenues to talk about deeper needs, paving the way toward gospel conversations.

Currency Detector

Our gospel currency needs to be genuine. True disciples of Jesus instinctively respond by loving people holistically. "For I was hungry and you gave me food, I was thirsty and you gave me drink, I was a stranger and you welcomed me, I was naked and you clothed me, I was sick and you visited me, I was in prison and you came to me" (Matt. 25:35–36). If we as individuals or as churches are not serving the needy, we can start by praying that the Spirit would show us a natural place to start. Usually we don't have to look far, but sometimes we can prayerfully and deliberately seek out places of need to make them part of our outreach strategy. Together we can ask God: "Where in our community could our church be salt and light, bringing true hope and change . . . and who will go?"

In asking for change, we also need to be ready to be changed ourselves. God may be challenging us to be the answer to our own prayer.

Investing Wisely

When the human tidal wave of refugees fleeing war and persecution crashed on German soil in 2015, many churches were quick to respond with physical aid, simply because it was the right thing to do: providing sleeping bags, food, and warm clothing. That was the easy part. However, we've heard on more than one occasion: "Germans love to give us things, but they don't want to be our friends." The cost of friendship is a lot higher. Investing time into relationships, which fosters a sense of trust and responsibility, is often much more important than assuaging our own guilty consciences by giving material goods.

Mehdi is a young husband and father of two very small children. I desperately wanted to buy him a double stroller, but after hesitating a bit, his answer was, "No, I want to be the one to buy it! What I need is help navigating eBay to look for a second-hand stroller. Would you be willing to help me do that?" I could see the joy well up in him at the idea of providing for his family, and I was convicted that my way of helping, though easy enough for me, would not have been dignifying to him. It takes wisdom from God to determine what level of response is appropriate. A response proportionate to the level of need maximizes gospel opportunities.

The refugee crisis, though certainly very tragic, has become a natural opportunity to reach out practically and share the good news, starting the conversation with issues such as loss of home and family, pain and suffering, hopes and dreams, evil and retribution. One very moving moment in our baptismal class was when we were studying the story of Abraham's calling to leave his home behind. Refugees talked about their desire to gain Christ in the face of their material and relational losses. They were starting to understand that God's plan for them had included physical hardships in order that they might grasp his love and mercy. There wasn't a dry eye in the room!

Banking on God

Sometimes we cannot help people because of personal limitations or realities outside of our control. In such cases, we will be stretched in our own faith, but this is good because we can point people to the one who can truly help them, the only one they can ultimately bank on. Even in small things, we must resist taking the place of God in their life and model God-dependency instead.

A missionary team was at a refugee home on a cold winter day when they encountered a man wearing no shoes. A young woman on the team noticed and spoke to him—"Jesus can give you shoes, you know?"—and prayed about this need with him. Several hours later, he chased the team down the street, holding a bag a random stranger had brought him. It was filled with shoes his size. He exclaimed, "I want Jesus in my heart!" And within minutes, he was sharing Jesus with another person on the street! It would have been easy to say, "Come with me, I'll buy you a pair of shoes," but that would have preempted an opportunity for him to experience Jesus's personal, merciful care. Instead, the young woman had the faith to challenge this now brother to trust Jesus as his provider too. Jesus's answer delighted the man and opened his heart to want to follow Christ.

Mutual Fund

Being in the position of helping people is a blessing, but it brings with it the temptation to pride and superiority. True love means humbly acknowledging our mutual need. I can honestly say I have greatly needed the perspective of our refugee friends on suffering, community, and the power of God to protect and provide. We need them to tell us about our cultural blind spots; we need their sensitivity to God's Spirit, their courage in the face of persecution, their rebuke of our apathy! When such new converts join a church, it is our obligation to become dependent on them for their unique gifts and God-given perspective. This is true of every person who becomes a part of Christ's body.

Nik Ripken, a veteran missionary and leading expert on the persecuted church, describes a time when he was interviewing nationals about what made a good missionary. He kept getting the same answer everywhere: "We don't know what makes a good missionary, but we can tell you the name of the man we love. . . . You want to know why we love him? He needs us. The rest of you have never needed us."[16] The people we serve will know we really love them when we start to need them.

BOTTOM LINE

Proclamation and mercy are inextricably bound in the person of Jesus Christ, our eternal Redeemer. How do we know this? God's currency of word and mercy came together most meaningfully at the cross. "Mercy and truth are met together; righteousness and peace have kissed each other" (Ps. 85:10 ASV). There, God's purchasing power was unleashed. The depth of his mercy was displayed in the sacrifice of his beloved Son, the Word of God incarnate, to redeem us from our deepest spiritual suffering—to meet our most primary need, reconciliation with God through purification from sin. Simultaneously, Jesus's physical death and resurrection set in motion the final redemption of our broken physical reality.

One day our souls and our bodies will be fully healed. We will be like Christ. God's glorious, resurrected children will enter a real promised land to enjoy the new heavens and the new earth in our new, flesh-and-blood resurrection bodies—spiritual bodies! (1 Cor. 15:44). We will live there in perfect community, and God's glorious presence will be our greatest delight. God's investment will be complete. What a privilege for us, desperate and needy people, to call others like ourselves to experience such a salvation and to join us in the joyous procession headed to the marriage supper of the Lamb!

PART 2

REPRESENTATIVE CONTEXTS

5

Spreading the Word in Everyday Life

Gloria Furman

It is a serious thing to live in a society of possible gods and god-
desses, to remember that the dullest and most uninteresting person
you can talk to may one day be a creature which, if you saw it now,
you would be strongly tempted to worship, or else a horror and
a corruption such as you now meet, if at all, only in a nightmare.

C. S. *Lewis,* The Weight of Glory[1]

Evangelism has an expiration date.

The story of the Bible reveals that evangelism is not eternal. It is
a means to an end, and that end is fellowship with God forever. No
two conversations, no two train rides, no two lunch breaks, and no
two walks at the park are the same. History is going somewhere.
Time is literally running out.

The day is coming when Jesus will wipe away every tear from

our eyes. There will be no more death, mourning, crying, or pain in the new creation; they are all "former things" that will pass away when Christ returns and the dwelling place of God will be with man (Rev. 21:3–4). In that day, evangelism will also become a "former thing." We can't circle a date on our calendar, but we can count on it coming soon. In fact, no one knows the day and hour, not even the angels of heaven, nor the Son, but the Father only (Matt. 24:36). So until the appointed day comes, we spend our days inviting our lost brothers and sisters to come home through faith in Christ who died, who lives, and who is coming again.

This is easy to say but so hard to remember and live, I know. All of us have a self-centered inward focus (naturally); we need God's intervention to give us a gospel-centered outward focus (supernaturally). We need God's help to lift our eyes and see that we are surrounded by dead people who desperately need us to preach the gospel and live out the life of Christ in their midst. Today is a Wednesday morning, and while I write about the cosmos-altering gospel of Jesus Christ, my mind lurches back and forth between prioritizing my to-do list and an urgent need to collate the shopping list for school supplies for my four kids. (Who has time to track down all this stuff?) I'm often tempted to live as if there is a disparity between my calling as an evangelist and my role as a woman with multiple hats to wear and roles to play. How can I reach out to my friends and neighbors in the middle of all that I have to do in my everyday life? Perhaps you can relate to feeling this imaginary tension.

My goals in this chapter are to remind us how God has strategically designed our everyday lives to be bursting with opportunities to joyfully spread the gospel, and to demonstrate how he gives us what we need to walk by faith in that endeavor.

ARE YOU DISTURBED BY YOUR LACK OF FAITH?

What does it mean to make the best use of the time while we sojourn on this earth among our lost brothers and sisters? There aren't enough whiteboards in the world to write down the bullet-pointed lists of practical means we have to share the good news. Last year the women's ministry of our church facilitated several evangelism-training workshops over the course of six weeks. We met in small groups ranging from five to fifteen women (depending on the week). Each group met once to discuss various Scripture passages concerning evangelism and to brainstorm practical means of integrating biblical truths into our everyday lives. During the portion of our meetings spent poring over the Bible text, extended minutes of thoughtful meditation were punctuated by affirming "Mmhmms," followed by pauses where the only noise was the air conditioner humming. (If you've ever led a small group, you've probably had times where the group was so silent that you've wondered if you need to interrupt the silence with words to keep the agenda moving along.) For all our times together of silent wonder at God's Word, when it came time for the groups to contribute their ideas of putting faith into action, my hand cramped up from writing so fast on the whiteboard.

When we stop and think about it long enough, we all know that God has strategically designed our everyday lives to be bursting with opportunities to spread his gospel. It isn't difficult to dream up ways we can practically order our priorities, adjust our schedules, and acquire any resources we need to live lifestyles of evangelism. Spreading the Word naturally fits into our everyday lives because God has arranged it all that way. After six weeks of recording the ideas from these diverse groups of women from dozens of countries and all walks of life, I concluded that we are certainly not lacking in the creativity and practicality departments!

In my reflections on this evangelism-training season, one consistent issue kept popping up. It was a snag in the system of implementation, so to speak. When we all considered what it might look like to implement some of these sensible ways to spread the Word, two things were missing: faith and wisdom. Our blood pressure nervously rises, butterflies flip-flop in our tummies, and pupils dilate with fear when we envision ourselves actually stepping into that conversation at work or hosting that Christmas party for the neighbor kids (for example). Perhaps you can relate to feeling faithless and uncertain when it comes to a lifestyle of evangelism? If so, I want to encourage you with some good news. Faith and wisdom are gifts from God! On one hand, we ought to be utterly disturbed by our lack of faith and wisdom. On the other hand, we need to consider our creatureliness and weakness and assume that of course we need more faith and wisdom. That's okay. We can ask God for all we need in order to do whatever it is he has called us to do, and he will give it to us in the time and way he deems best to glorify himself as he provides for his children.

WHAT DO OUR LOST FRIENDS NEED?

Faith and wisdom are necessary components to spreading the Word in our everyday lives. As already mentioned, practical habits and ideas are a dime a dozen. We need faith to believe that God is the one doing the work of evangelism through us, and wisdom to see this truth played out all around us whether or not we take notice. Perhaps you've drawn "The Bridge" illustration for someone at a coffee shop; or you've explained "Two Ways to Live" to a colleague; or you've outlined "God, Man, Christ, Response" in conversations with your children; or you've sent Bibles and apologetics books to your relatives for every birthday, Christmas, and Easter.[2] (A friend of mine has noticed that the stack of gift books on his mother's bedside table has risen so high she can no longer safely rest her tea on it.) Perhaps you have written the names of your loved ones on index cards and taped them to your bathroom mirror to remind you to pray. You're hopeful that your light is shining brightly enough before your neighbors down the street that they may see your good works and give glory to your Father who is in heaven (Matt. 5:16). (You're hopeful that the housewife in the apartment next door was not home to hear the latest verbal spat with your teenagers.) Maybe you volunteer at the visitors table at church when you haven't brought someone yourself. When it comes to being ready to tackle objections, you've taken a class or read a book to help you become well versed in the basics of the religions represented in your neighborhood. Preparing to do the work of an evangelist is something all believers can do.

I mention all of this to further demonstrate that we are not lacking in the creativity and practicality departments when it comes to everyday evangelism. All over God's world, faithful believers are making efforts to share the gospel in such a way that lost men and women do not suffer from ignorance of the truth. There is no question that the church can clearly explain the gospel and aptly defend and adorn it! From the Patristics to the Reformers and beyond, we've inherited a tradition of outstanding gospel clarity and corporate witness based in God's living and active Word.

The faithful evangelism of the church is gradually removing the obstacle of ignorance from Sri Lanka to Seattle. But ignorance is not the deepest issue. People are perishing forever in hell because *they refused to love the truth* and so be saved (2 Thess. 2:10). It may be that your friend from playgroup can recite the gospel back to you perfectly and has done the "Christianity Explored" course twice at two different churches. Your lost preteen may be raised in your gospel-announcing, grace-embodying home and not remember a day when he didn't hear about Jesus and the salvation God offers to him by faith through grace—yet still be darkened in his understanding, alienated from the life of God *"because of the ignorance that is in them, due to their hardness of heart"* (Eph. 4:18). At the end of the day, you cannot grab hold of the eyelids of someone's spiritually blind eyes and pry them open to see the Truth. Only the Spirit of God can do that.

Since Satan, the god of this world, has blinded the minds of unbelievers, they cannot see the light of the gospel of the glory of Christ (2 Cor. 4:4). Though the gospel shines like daylight, the blind will continue to stumble in the dark unless God himself opens their eyes. I remind you of this, not to discourage you but to help you rely on the God who raises the dead. *God raises the dead!* By faith we affirm with the apostle Paul, "For I am not ashamed of the gospel, for it is the power of God for salvation to everyone who believes, to the Jew first and also to the Greek" (Rom. 1:16). Don't be disturbed by your lack of faith—believe God! By faith you were saved out of a lost world, by faith you live among lost people, and by faith you can preach the gospel in the everyday life that God has designed for you.

DON'T FORGET WHAT THEY ALREADY KNOW

They already know about God—everyone does. Scripture plainly teaches that God has revealed himself to the world through what he has made, but that in their unrighteousness, people suppress the truth (Rom. 1:18–23). Every single person you meet has the capacity to know God in a saving way and has been given ample evidence of God's invisible attributes, and yet all people lack the ability to know God in a saving way through their own devices. That's why the word of the cross must be preached—the gospel must be shared. We need to remember this about our lost friends: they already know something of God, and they instinctively know that they are truly, ultimately unsatisfied with whatever they have replaced him with. Augustine put it this way: "You have made us for yourself, O Lord, and our hearts are restless until they rest in you."[3] Our friends have restless hearts, and as we go about our everyday lives, we can point this out to them with the Spirit's help.

The plate of fresh dates was full when we started our conversation across my living room coffee table. I listened as my friend shared about her new business venture, the online meditation class she was taking to combat her stress, and the litany of tasks facing her that week. I prayed for God to open my friend's eyes and help her see her need for him. The Spirit prompted me to ask her a question: "And then, what?" And then I waited for her answer. She waited for her answer too as her eyes widened and squinted, her mind searching for what it was she was searching for.

"Then what?" is a motive-revealing question, slicing through the layers of flurried religious activity our hearts conjure up as we suppress the truth of God. (Even our self-proclaimed "nonreligious" friends, as my friend in this story claimed to be, engage in the religious endeavor of exchanging the glory of God for other things.) *What are you looking for? Do you realize your heart is looking for something? How will you know when you have found it? Can you trust your heart and its desires? All of us, the world over, want to be happy. What (or Who!) do you think can satisfy the desires of every human heart?* Because we understand from Scripture that every unbelieving person we meet knows of God yet doesn't know God, our motive-revealing questions can turn on the proverbial light switch in a room, highlighting to our friends the fact that for all of their industrious and religious heart following, they are yet sitting in darkness.

We can also ask doubt-casting questions like "Really?" when our friends give us answers that they themselves know are insufficient. "I believe we can all reach god in our own ways and it doesn't matter." *Oh?* "After school starts and I have my days back and the kids have their routines, then we'll all be much happier." *Really?* (I've been asking myself this doubt-casting question lately too!) These are questions related to everyday matters—our goings and our comings—and the Spirit of God is always present to help us discuss them. God has, after all, strategically designed our everyday lives for the spread of his glory into every living room, ferryboat, shoe store, homeless shelter, beach, and birthday party in this world.

The alleged awkwardness of discussing spiritual things in the course of our everyday, so-called "secular" lives truly pales in comparison to the public spectacle of our crucified Lord. To use a colloquial metaphor, the "elephant in the room" of man's rebellion against our Creator is hiding in plain sight. Often when I ask someone, "What will you do with your sin?" the discomfort they feel at that thought betrays their verbal commitment to secularism. God, in his rich kindness, demonstrates his forbearance and patience through persistent messengers who are willing to bring up seemingly awkward subjects such as sin and the wrath of God. Just as his rich mercy reached out for us, so God's patient kindness is meant to lead our friends to repentance (Rom. 2:4). Vertically challenged Zacchaeus climbed a tree because he felt he needed to see Jesus for some reason (Luke 19:1–8); the Ethiopian eunuch was "randomly" pondering Isaiah 53 during his commute (Acts 8:26–40); Sergius Paulus, a highly educated official, asked Paul to bring him God's Word (Acts 13:7–8); and a Roman jailer was set free after he begged Paul to tell him what he must do to be saved (Acts 16:25–34). The Spirit of the Lord is at work in the world. You and I never know who has been, who is, and who will soon be wrestling with these weighty spiritual issues, waiting for someone to bring them God's Word.

DON'T FORGET HE GAVE YOU A MESSAGE FOR THEM

A friend of mine likes to say, "The best gospel presentation is the one given." All of us may not have been given "the gift of evangelism," but all of us have been given a job to do of spreading the Word. Specifically, we have been given a ministry of reconciliation. We who have had the venom of that fiery Serpent flow through our veins since birth have now gazed upon the bronze serpent suspended and hanging in the wilderness outside the camp . . . and lived! Only because of God's mercy do we have the assurance of Christ's confidence in his sacrifice for sins, as he has said: "And I, when I am lifted up from the earth, will draw all people to myself" (John 12:32). As you go about your everyday life, never forget that while you are indeed walking among the lost, there *are* some who are being saved. Jesus has other sheep and he must bring them also. Christ himself assures us that "they will listen to my voice" (John 10:16). Only God knows if the person seated next to you at the soccer game is being drawn to the Lord by his Spirit, and if her thirst for living water has been piqued; to those people the word of the cross doesn't sound ridiculous—it's the very power of God (1 Cor. 1:18)! The message of the cross is no mere history lesson or moralistic maxim—it is the power of God. The living church now dwells on the earth, a temple of God's presence spreading to every cubicle, ranch, hut, and condo on the globe. Our work here is gloriously clear-cut and distinct: we are ambassadors with a message.

> Therefore, if anyone is in Christ, he is a new creation. The old has passed away; behold, the new has come. All this is from God, who through Christ reconciled us to himself and gave us the ministry of reconciliation; that is, in Christ God was reconciling the world to himself, not counting their trespasses against them, and entrusting to us the message of reconciliation. Therefore, we are ambassadors for Christ, God making his appeal through us. We implore you on behalf of Christ, be reconciled to God. For our sake he made him to be sin who knew no sin, so that in him we might become the righteousness of God. (2 Cor. 5:17–21)

Through us! God is making his appeal to this lost world through us. What King would take former traitors like us and turn them into his loyal ambassadors? Where I live, in a global city, we regularly drive past the consulates and embassies of various countries. My kids like to notice the distinct architectural styles; how big and tall their flag is flying; how long is the line of people waiting outside for consular services; and whether or not armed guards are standing sentinel on the sidewalk.

One time we needed visa services from the embassy of a country we planned to visit. I parked our minivan on the street right next to a two-story, white villa in between a dentist's office and someone's house. The GPS said we had arrived, but we weren't sure. The building wasn't decorated like the other embassies we had seen before. I got out of the car, jogged a few meters, and noticed a parking cone with a paper sign on it—"Parking for the Embassy." It didn't seem like it, but we really were in the right place. What mattered was not the appearance of a "typical" embassy but the presence of the ambassador inside with the authority to speak and act on behalf of her country. Incidentally, the ambassador denied our visa requests that day based on a paperwork technicality. My husband tried to negotiate the faulty paperwork, but she dismissed us with simple but clear words: "It is because of the laws of the country that I cannot issue you this visa." It wasn't her job to assuage our disappointment, because she was just the messenger. (We got the visas later when we refiled the right papers.)

Too often in our evangelistic efforts the role we try to embody is that of an educator (e.g., expertly teaching lost people about Christian values and behavior) rather than that of an ambassador. We resist opportunities to spread the Word because we do not deem ourselves professional-enough or educated-enough teachers, so we pass on these conversations and rationalize that we weren't the best-suited Christian to educate that lost person. But an ambassador's job is different. An ambassador is to faithfully relate the message from her King to those to whom she has been sent. She doesn't deceitfully change the message or "compassionately" hide it from people who need to be reconciled to God. The gospel belongs to God (Rom. 1:1–6). This relaying of a message presumes that the ambassador *knows* the message of the one who has sent her, and this is *the* message she communicates through her words and consistent lifestyle.

DON'T FORGET HE IS ALWAYS SENDING YOU

So the ambassador must know the message, articulate it clearly and faithfully, and remember that she is never "off duty." We are ambassadors for Christ whether or not we are always conscious of the fact. We do not clock out of being ambassadors when we enter our kids' bedroom, nor when we leave our front door.

I received a phone call from the school's health clinic one time (okay, many times), and this time I had to come pick up one of my kids per school policy concerning fevers. Her fever was 0.1 over the acceptable temperature. "Seriously? 0.1?" I grumbled to myself. I had planned strategic ministry for that morning. When I sat with my child at the doctor's office, I was busy texting the friends I needed to reschedule, and a nurse started asking me questions about where I went to church. She kept asking about where our church meets and what time it starts, and then when she said, "I want to come to your church . . ." the light bulb finally lit up in my head and I truly joined the conversation. I put down my phone and realized that God had used my child's ear infection as part of his plan to send his ambassador to this doctor's office to see this nurse. From before time began, he planned these good works for me to walk in, and I had only been aware of my own plans. I was also reminded that day not to assume that God isn't in labor over someone's new life in Christ. (And don't assume you need to feel spiritually "on your game" in order for God to use you in evangelism.)

God's plans for his ambassadors are always most strategically aligned with his mission to spread his fame. We may imagine that we have sent ourselves to the grocery store at bedtime because someone drank the last of the milk and we need to eat breakfast in the morning, but all of our comings and goings have been designed by the God who spoke mask-eyed raccoons and cellular mitosis into existence.

On a related note, in recent years I have become more impressed by the fact that all of God's calling, equipping, and sending occurs in view of the watching cosmos. The manifold wisdom of God is being made known to the rulers and authorities in the heavenly places as his church is being called out of darkness (Eph. 3:10).

The gospel turns traitors into ambassadors and guests into cohosts. Invite your friends and neighbors in—go out and run to meet them. When you step out of bed in the morning, when you walk through a parking lot at work, when you wander the aisles of a store, remember you are an ambassador—a "cohost" of sorts. Christian hospitality cannot be contained within the walls of your individual home; "this is *our Father's world*—oh, let us ne'er forget!"[4] And what does a cohost do? She introduces his guests to *him*. "Come, see a man who told me all that I ever did. Can this be the Christ?" (John 4:29). One by one, individuals are raised to new life in Christ when the Spirit causes them to be born again and they embrace the gospel. What a privilege we have to be sent as his ambassadors to our lost brothers and sisters!

Perhaps you have heard the phrase "Cut her and she bleeds Bible." It's an expression describing a person committed to living by every word that proceeds from the mouth of God: every word spoken gives grace to those who hear.

A friend of mine likes to share what she read that morning in her Bible with the people she encounters as she goes about her day. She simply overflows.

Another friend pays for her decaf lattes and chocolate croissants at the cafe she frequents (the chocolate croissants I understand, but the decaf I do not), sits down at a table, and then when the server brings out her order, explains that she is about to pray for her meal and asks, "What can I pray for you?"

Rebecca physically hands people her open Bible or her smartphone with the Bible app open on it when she is talking to someone about what she is learning or reading, and they read (and many times, keep reading).

"How was your weekend?" is a question that Sheila asks at work every week, and when it's her turn, she talks about the sermon she heard at church.

My friend Kamella asks people to listen to her Scripture memory recitation for the day to help double check her memory (and spread the Word!).

Gina is a storyteller. She says she receives the most requests for repeat rehearsals of stories about Jesus and his interactions with women in the Bible. Talking about the Word that is our very lives (Deut. 32:47) is, naturally, something the Spirit leads Word-dependent, Word-filled women to do.

Merely being friendly to people is not evangelism; spreading the Word of truth, the gospel, is evangelism. Good thoughts about us or our family or our church cannot save anyone, but only faith in Christ. Scripture is clear: "So faith comes from hearing, and hearing through the word of Christ" (Rom. 10:17). Whatever it is we call the activity we are doing—sharing good news, witnessing, spreading the Word, teaching the gospel—it must communicate the word of Christ. Our word and message carry no authority, only Christ's. Our word and message are devoid of power to save, only Christ's. In Christ, God is reconciling the world to himself, not counting their trespasses against them! God has entrusted to us this message of reconciliation. Yes, make lists for a grocery run, show up at the homeowners' association meeting, schedule the appointments, catch the subway, renew your driver's license, and do what you need to do, but go knowing you are being sent by God as an ambassador. The passionate, committed, resilient imploring that we do is not for our own sakes, to build our own reputations among women as "nice people"—it is on behalf of Jesus Christ himself, who hung on a cross and was made to be sin for us. May the measure of our boldness in deciding to know nothing among our neighbors except Jesus Christ and him crucified (1 Cor. 2:2) correspond to the indomitable power and promise of Jesus to be with us in this endeavor.

ONE LAST THING

I haven't yet told you the recipe for the secret sauce. In all of these exhortations to joyfully spread the Word in our everyday lives,

I have found one thing absolutely critical. My friend Lillian is a seasoned veteran in helping to train others in the work of evangelism. I asked her to summarize the way she co-led these trainings with her husband in the churches where they served. First they asked for volunteers who would be willing to come forward and wear a traditional outfit of someone from a different cultural background. Several volunteers would stand at the front dressed in various clothing articles from different countries of the world, representing multiple world religions. The point of the training was to reveal "the most effective thing to say to start an evangelistic conversation in everyday life" with these people. Lillian assured everyone present that even though these representative people were from different backgrounds, this one method was a surefire way to get started talking about the gospel with any and all of them. One lone person was delegated to stand at the front, facing forward and holding up the poster board that contained "the answer," hidden from view. Finally, Lillian or her husband would say, "We are now going to learn *the most effective thing to say* in order to start an evangelistic conversation. Are you ready?" And that person would turn around to show everyone the poster. It simply read "Hello." In whatever language you speak, your *hello* could initiate the first conversation among hundreds (or even the very last in the line) that God uses to snatch someone from the ever-approaching reality of eternal damnation in hell. It is such a small word to utter, and it only requires a mustard seed of faith in our great God for it to pass over our vocal cords, doesn't it?

It is fitting that God would use such feeble words from the lips of feeble creatures to carry out his extraordinary mission on the earth. The throne room in heaven reverberates with unceasing praise as "beautiful feet" (Rom. 10:15) run through everyday lives with God's good news of great joy that is for all the people.

6

Spreading the Word among Children

Jamie Love

To Timothy, my beloved child, . . . I am reminded of your sincere faith, a faith that dwelt first in your grandmother Lois and your mother Eunice and now, I am sure, dwells in you as well. . . . Continue in what you have learned and have firmly believed, knowing from whom you learned it and how from childhood you have been acquainted with the sacred writings, which are able to make you wise for salvation through faith in Christ Jesus.

2 Timothy 1:2, 5; 3:14–15

The very word *evangelism* causes many Christians to shudder. I am not sure why, but perhaps it is because they remember, from years gone by, the high-pressure sales pitch and closing that passed for so-called "soul winning." Or maybe it was the "share your faith" class where you were expected to be a seminary graduate in order to present the gospel accurately and you knew your Greek was not up for the job. Possibly it was the going out "two by two," cold-calling, door-to-door evangelism that makes so many people shy away from any discussion on gospel witness.

Evangelism seems to be even more challenging when children are the target audience. Maybe they are too young to understand. It would be better (easier) just to simply wait until they come to us with questions. I would much rather live the faith in front of them, letting my lifestyle be the catalyst for their believing in Jesus. After all, we should not force our faith upon them, should we?

My aim in this chapter is to spur you on in evangelism among children. My hope is to assure you of God's calling and enabling for the blessed privilege he has assigned to all believers whom he has entrusted with children, and to all who have been incorporated into the body of Christ. This privilege of bringing good news to the youngest souls among us actually belongs to all of us.

THE CALL

In the context of modern family planning and our illusions of control over fertility, it is hard to remember that all children exist by the sovereign hand of an almighty God. That child, those children, have been entrusted to you and to the church by God. They belong to God—evangelize them! They are not mere boys and girls, but someday men and women, now under your influence—evangelize them! Their being is not merely temporary but eternal—evangelize them! Those young ones, as needy as they may appear, possess minds and souls that you have been given the awesome privilege and responsibility to train both for time and eternity—evangelize them!

Reader, such is your dignity and honor. Embrace and value your rich calling to evangelize the sons and daughters of the almighty God and help them understand that all of the Scripture points to his Son Jesus Christ:

And beginning with Moses and all the Prophets, he interpreted to them in all the Scriptures the things concerning himself. . . . "Thus it is written, that the Christ should suffer and on the third day rise from the dead, and that repentance for the forgiveness of sins should be proclaimed in his name to all nations. . . . You are witnesses of these things. (Luke 24:27, 46–48)

And there is salvation in no one else, for there is no other name under heaven given among men by which we must be saved. (Acts 4:12)

Cherish God's providence that your home and church are "the cradle in which children are nurtured so that each one will find their place in the kingdom of God."[1] Treasure your honored position to prepare those who will one day dwell in the heavenly home that Christ has gone to prepare (John 14:1–3).

THE CHARGE

In one long-used child dedication ceremony,[2] the pastor addresses the parent(s) with this joyful but solemn charge:

The divine-human task of developing a personality after the birth of a Child is the most delicate and serious work to which man is called. All the sights and sounds that play upon the sensitive little body help to determine his future characteristics. The love of the home affects the Child in a thousand ways for good. As the Child grows he may perceive the spiritual life of his parents as a rose drinks in the sunlight. The religious conversation of a mother with her Child, even at a very tender age, will make for his fuller and richer growth. . . .

It is your duty, therefore, to receive this Child from God's hand and to teach him to know and love God, and, working in obedience to God's will, to help in the unfolding of the Child's spiritual life. From your example the Child must learn to pray. From your example he must learn to read and love the Bible, and from your example he must learn the way of fellowship with Christ.

Above all you are to make it your constant prayer and effort to lead the Child to know and love Christ so that when he comes to the age of proper understanding he will . . . confess Christ as his Savior, . . . obey him, and . . . give himself in loyal and loving service as a member of the church, which is the body of Christ.

Consider the biblical illustration of this charge lived out in the lives of a faithful grandmother and mother. The apostle Paul writes these words to young Pastor Timothy:

I am reminded of your sincere faith, a faith that dwelt first in your grandmother Lois and your mother Eunice and now, I am sure, dwells in you as well. . . . But as for you, continue in what you have learned and have firmly believed, knowing from whom you learned it and how from childhood you have been acquainted with the sacred writings, which are able to make you wise for salvation through faith in Christ Jesus. (2 Tim. 1:5; 3:14–15)

Sometimes when we encounter characters in Scripture, that is really all they are to us—characters—devoid of real life. This is a great mistake. The women Paul mentions, Lois and Eunice, are very much like you and me. Their stories and struggles are real.

They were partakers of the same sinful nature as the one whom they had to train, encompassed with all the weakness of fallen humanity, and subject to all its temptations. They had to contend against their own sinful tendencies; to watch over their own spirits; to strive with their own waywardness; and in the midst of all this, to set before their child, their grandchild, an example of patience, forbearance, and holy living, that is a true and faithful commentary on the sacred truths they are to teach.[3]

Lois and Eunice in the midst of a complicated home and corrupt culture raised up godly Timothy (Acts 16:1–3). The presence of Timothy's unbelieving father and the pressures of an ungodly culture did not dampen his grandmother's and mother's faith or their trust in God's Word. They pressed their faith into Timothy and committed their boy to the Lord they trusted. They saturated Timothy's heart with the "sacred writings, which are able to make you wise for salvation through faith in Christ Jesus" (2 Tim. 3:15). And they clearly brought him into the regular fellowship, worship, and teaching of the believers around them.

Lois's and Eunice's offspring, Timothy, after whom two New Testament books are named, was a third-generation Christian (2 Tim. 1:5). He was spoken well of by the believers at Lystra and Iconium (Acts 16:2). Timothy was pivotal in the formation of the early church in the days of the apostles and a companion to the apostle Paul. He was commended by Paul: "For I have no one like him, who will be genuinely concerned for your welfare. For they all seek their own interests, not those of Jesus Christ. But you know Timothy's proven worth, how as a son with a father he has served with me in the gospel" (Phil. 2:20–22).

Timothy, the child who became the man of God, did not get there without the foundational labor of his grandmother Lois and mother, Eunice. In order for children to find their place in God's kingdom, God uses the joyful surrender of believers around them to the mission of evangelizing them on God's behalf.

So let us learn from these faithful women of old and "consider the outcome of their way of life, and imitate their faith" (Heb. 13:7). Let us believe as Lois and Eunice did that Jesus Christ will continue to raise up boys and girls into men and women of God as we introduce them to him. Let us share our Savior and seize the moments we have to prepare young souls for time and for eternity. We can trust, like Lois and Eunice, that our work in evangelizing children will echo throughout the ages for the good of their souls, the glory of God, the praise of Christ, and the edification of his church.

YOUR BLESSED OPPORTUNITY

Hearing Cries for a Savior

As a mother and grandmother, I am sure the birth of Timothy brought great joy to Lois and Eunice. I was present—in labor and delivery, *Phewwwww!*—for the births of most of my ten grandchildren. I have felt the wonder and excitement of welcoming a beautiful, bouncing baby into the world. What awe! What joy! What thankfulness! Witnessing the entrance of your offspring and knowing that God decided to use you to raise them up is absolutely incredible!

However, in the midst of the celebration of new life, we cannot lose sight of the task set before us. Lois and Eunice did not. They kept young Timothy's soul in view. As a result, they shared their faith with their child. And Paul became a spiritual father who continued to teach and mentor him. We believers are all called to the same labor, that of raising up the next generation to know and serve the Lord Jesus.

Lois's and Eunice's eternal perspective did not dim with the passing of time. Neither must ours. They understood that this work of the Lord would be "a long obedience in the same direction."[4] Therefore, they made it their aim in life to acquaint the child entrusted to them with the living and active Word of God. They probably spent many an afternoon or evening telling him the stories of Scripture. They probably sang songs from the Bible with him. They probably talked about Jesus as they were getting up in the morning and going out and coming in. They probably prayed with him and in front of him about all the joys and sorrows and needs of their lives, including the salvation of those around them who did not believe.

Lois and Eunice heard the true cry of young Timothy, the cry of his soul, and they responded by nursing him in their faith and feeding him with the Word. This cry was not unique to Timothy. It is an old cry. It is a familiar cry. It is a loud cry. It is a cry that will not be satisfied by anything in this world. It is the cry of "Just give me Jesus!"

It was the cry of Adam and Eve after the fall. Adam, the first man, by his single act of rebellion against God, plunged the entire human race into sin. As a result, Adam's offspring bear the marks of sin and death (Gen. 1:26–27; 2:15–16; 3:1–11; Rom. 5:12, 16, 18–19). But even as God declared the consequences of sin and death, he made a promise. He said to the Serpent: "I will put enmity between you and the woman, and between your offspring and her offspring; he shall bruise your head, and you shall bruise his heel" (Gen. 3:15). Ever since, fallen human beings have cried out for that offspring, the one who brings final victory over sin and death.

It was the cry of Eve as she looked for this great promise of God in her offspring Cain, saying, "I have gotten a man with the help of the LORD" (Gen. 4:1).

It was the cry of Lamech when he "called his name Noah, saying, 'Out of the ground that the LORD has cursed, this one shall bring us relief from our work and from the painful toil of our hands'" (Gen. 5:29).

It was the cry of Abraham when he extolled, "God will provide for himself the lamb for a burnt offering, my son" (Gen. 22:8).

It was the cry of Jacob when he prophesied,

Judah, your brothers shall praise you;
    your hand shall be on the neck of your enemies;
    your father's sons shall bow down before you.
Judah is a lion's cub;
    from the prey, my son, you have gone up. . . .
The scepter shall not depart from Judah, . . .
    and to him shall be the obedience of the peoples.
        (Gen. 49:8–10)

It was the cry of Moses, who exhorted, "The LORD your God will raise up for you a prophet like me from among you, from your brothers—it is to him you shall listen" (Deut. 18:15).

It was the cry of David as he prayed, "Who am I, O Lord GOD, and what is my house, that you have brought me thus far? And yet this was a small thing in your eyes, O Lord GOD. You have spoken also of your servant's house for a great while to come, and this is instruction for mankind, O Lord GOD!" (2 Sam. 7:18–19).

It was the cry of the apostle John:

Then I saw in the right hand of him who was seated on the throne a scroll . . . sealed with seven seals. And I saw a mighty angel proclaiming with a loud voice, "Who is worthy to open the scroll and break its seals?" And no one in heaven or on earth or under the earth was able to open the scroll or to look into it, and I began to weep loudly because no one was found worthy to open the scroll or to look into it. And one of the elders said to me, "Weep no more; behold, the Lion of the tribe of Judah, the Root of David, has conquered, so that he can open the scroll and its seven seals." . . .

I saw a Lamb standing, as though it had been slain. . . . He went and took the scroll from the right hand of him who was seated on the throne. And when he had taken the scroll, the four living creatures and the twenty-four elders fell down before the Lamb. . . . And they sang a new song, saying,

"Worthy are you to take the scroll
    and to open its seals,
for you were slain, and by your blood you ransomed
        people for God
    from every tribe and language and people and nation,
and you have made them a kingdom and priests to
        our God,
    and they shall reign on the earth."

. . . before the foundation of the world . . . the Lamb who was slain. (Rev. 5:1–10; 13:8)

It was my cry. I praise God that my mother, *my* Eunice, heard it and "gave me Jesus!" I am forever grateful that she was undistracted by the noise of her own inadequacies. She was undaunted by the pressures of a complicated home. She was unyielding in her resolve to have me in the congregation of God's people so that I could hear the preacher proclaim the good news of what God has done for us through Christ.

In that congregation were spiritual aunts and uncles and grandmothers and grandfathers who taught me to know and trust God's Word—and who lovingly showed me how to live it out among the body of Christ. Forty-five years removed, I am still benefiting from the godly example of Ms. Edwards. She was one of the reasons that favorite TV show, *Soul Train*, was cut short every third Saturday of the month—as I raced to be on time for the youth meeting she cosupervised at our church. Ms. Edwards's love of the Word, love of children, and faithfulness to the local church made a lasting impression upon me. She graciously, patiently, and sacrificially gave of her life and resources to ensure that I saw the beauty and splendor of Jesus Christ. She was a real, practical example of how to love and serve Christ. She passed it on.

Not only did my mom hear my cry but, along with our church family, she also helped me recognize that same cry in my own children. She believed, "The promise is for you and for your children and for all who are far off, everyone whom the Lord our God calls to himself" (Acts 2:39). Her instruction to me was "Give them Jesus!" Praise God! He used me to evangelize my children. He allowed me to witness their new birth.

It is now the cry of my grandchildren. I hear it! Thanks to Lois and Eunice and my mom, I recognize it. I say to my children, on the strength of the witnesses that have gone before me, "Give them Jesus!" It is our prayer and eager anticipation as we, together with their parents and with fellow believers, "toil, struggling with all his energy that he powerfully works" in us (Col. 1:29), that God will indeed respond with the soul-satisfying Jesus.

Reader, it is the cry of your child's soul—and the cry of every young person God puts in your path. Do you hear it? It is a cry that nothing in this world will satisfy. Do not offer them material things that will only make them covetous. Do not offer them entertainment that will only dull their spiritual senses. Do not offer them the throne of your heart that will only teach them self-worship.

Their cry will only be satisfied as you "give them Jesus!" Oh! Be quick to offer your child "the food that endures to eternal life, which the Son of Man will give to you. . . . the bread of God . . . who comes down from heaven and gives life to the world" (John 6:27, 33). Be constant in satisfying their thirst with the one who said, "Whoever drinks of the water that I will give him will never be thirsty again. The water that I will give him will become in him a spring of water welling up to eternal life" (John 4:13–14).

As you share Jesus with children, be ever so diligent to feast on him yourself. That child is a perceptive witness of your own cravings. May children see in you the appetite of the psalmist who said, "How sweet are your words to my taste, sweeter than honey to my mouth!" (Ps. 119:103). As you savor Jesus while offering him to the young ones around you, they will be more inclined to "taste and see that the LORD is good" (Ps. 34:8).

By the good grace of God, may your child leave your home as Timothy left Lois and Eunice's home, as I left my mother's home, as my children left my home, singing:

Well of water ever springing,
Bread of life so rich and free,
Untold wealth that never faileth,
My Redeemer is to me.

Hallelujah! I have found Him
Whom my soul so long had craved!
Jesus satisfies my longings,
Thru' His blood I now am saved.[5]

Seize the Moment

Summer is one of my favorite times of the year.[6] It takes us past the blistery cold and blanketing snow of the winter. Summer gets us beyond the heavy rains and muddy grounds of spring. But better than this is the opportunity to spend concentrated time with the grandchildren. Each summer we are treated with the comings and goings of our children's children. At times we will have all ten.

You can imagine the busyness of giving each one the attention they have come to expect from their Granny (my name from the older ones) / GiGi (my name from the younger ones). The mounds of food that are consumed. The constant buzz of conversation. The barrage of questions. What some may see as mayhem to be avoided, I see as moments to be seized.

One of the traditions we have is to gather all the grandchildren one last time, before they depart for home, and ask each of them what they enjoyed most about their time with Papa and Granny/GiGi. Their answers amaze us every time we do this. What we thought was quite simple and insignificant meant the most to them. Here is how it goes:

"I liked it when we went to that big playground."

"I liked the cookout and bonfire at Uncle Stephen's and Aunt Mandy's."

"No, no the best thing was the UNO tournament!"

"Yeah that was cool, but I really enjoyed going to the different restaurants, especially Tom and Eddie's."

"I really liked riding around with Tia Nell and Vernon Hills Days."

Then it happens. One of them says something that lands right at the core of my heart: "I really liked the times we spent reading and talking about the Bible."

This response reminds me in an unexpected but fresh way of seizing the moment by spending time with the grandchildren in the Word of God. The other things we did with them were good and, I would say, important and certainly fun. But none of them was as important as the time in the Scripture—and they enjoyed it. Spending time with the next generations around the "sacred writings" is indeed serious business (2 Tim. 1:5; 3:14–15). Times of going to church, participating in family worship, and discussing the Scriptures with the children's friends are all moment-seizing opportunities.

Sometimes it is just as simple as being faithful to the Lord's Day worship. I was reminded of this one Sunday when my granddaughter was sitting next to me while we were receiving the Lord's Table. This five-year-old began a series of questions that even to this day, three years removed, stirs my soul. During the service, she wanted to know why the children could not "have any." I answered her question attempting to be as clear as I could, seizing the moment to tell how Jesus took on our sins and died in our place. Trusting Granny, she was content with my quick and short answer. However, knowing her, I was convinced she had other unanswered questions. I also wanted to spend more time with her, ensuring that she understood what I briefly shared during the Lord's Table. This is where she and I are so much alike: we both like being thorough.

Our opportunity to discuss her questions at length came during that evening's time of family worship. Toward the end of our Bible reading together, we give time for questions and answers. Even though I already knew, I specifically asked her if she had any more questions about the Lord's Table. Of course she did!

I am amazed at how just being faithful to the ABCs of Christian living, such as attending church, can have such a profound evangelistic impact upon children. Many are the stories of children who came to know Christ because kind neighbors took them along to church. Because we took our grandchildren to church with us, I had yet another opportunity to share the gospel with my young granddaughter, not once but twice in one day. These opportunities came because this little girl observed us in worship, and as Moses wrote in Exodus 12:26, she asked, "What do you mean by this service?"

What is really amazing is that I am talking about my grand-children. Where did all the time go? It does not seem that long ago when I was spending time with their parents and their friends when they were young.

Life is like a summer in Midwestern America. It is brief. It will not be long before fall begins to set in and the green turns to yellow, red, and orange. Then, in a few short months, the grass and the trees will quietly—almost without notice—fall asleep for the winter. That is how life is, according to James 4:14. We do not have much time to evangelize the children God brings into our lives. Seizing the moment is indeed the order of the day.

God entrusts parents and also whole congregations with the blessing of children. May we hear and respond to the call of the prophet Jeremiah: "Arise, cry out. . . ! Pour out your heart like water before the presence of the Lord! Lift your hands to him for the lives of your children" (Lam. 2:19).

Gladly accept that child, those children, from the hand of God. Earnestly pray for the salvation of their souls. Acquaint them with the Scriptures, the only thing that will make them wise unto salvation. Give them Jesus!

If this is your commitment, if this is your plea, then I say, in the words of the wise Bishop J. C. Ryle: "I have a good hope that you will indeed train up your children well—train well for this life and train well for the life to come; train well for earth and train well for heaven; train them for God, for Christ, and for eternity."[7]

Spreading the Word among University Students

SharDavia Walker

Our greatest affliction is not anxiety, or even guilt, but rather homesickness—a nostalgia or ineradicable yearning to be at home with God.

Donald Bloesch, Theological Notebook

THE BEAUTY OF THE MESSAGE

Think back to a time when you felt far away from home. Maybe it was for a day, or a year—or longer. Maybe you have been welcomed home with a loving embrace from a parent or parent figure, friend, roommate, or spouse. Or perhaps you long for a home where you might experience that kind of welcome and love. The comfort, familiarity, and sense of belonging that we associate with home are undeniable.

I have recently come to view the regeneration that happens when a person accepts and believes the gospel as a sort of "coming home."

During my first year of college, I was finding my way in a sea of strangers on a beautiful campus in rural southwestern Virginia. While I studied the newness and diversity of the leaves' colors that first fall, walking to class, I internally longed for the familiarity and safety of my hometown. After spending weeks with strangers, finally walking through the front door of my parents' home to enjoy the comforts of my childhood bed and to eat a home-cooked meal around the dinner table was satisfying to my heart.

Not all students share my eagerness to return to the familiarity of home—and, indeed, there is a far greater return home than a blissful break from a college or university campus.[1] Coming to faith in Jesus is like coming home to a place we have always wanted but never knew we desired. Before our redemption, we are unknowingly homesick for a land—or better yet, a person—we have never seen or known but whose absence we still sense. Coming to faith is like the warm embrace of a beloved parent as we excitedly run into the arms of the Father. Our soul finally breathes a sigh of relief, saying, "This is home. This is where I was meant to be. This is where I belong."

In the well-known parable Jesus told in Luke 15:11–32, we encounter a boy who has, in so many words, wished his father dead, hastily taken his inheritance, and squandered it on the world's pleasures. After realizing his desperate situation, he resolves to return to his father, hoping that at best he will treat him as one of the hired servants. Surprisingly, "while he [the son] was still a long way off, his father saw him and felt compassion, and ran and embraced him and kissed him" (Luke 15:20). It sounds like that father was on the lookout, awaiting his son's return. I imagine there was a longing in the father's heart to be reunited with his son. The father welcomes him home with open arms and a warm embrace that the son surely longed for but certainly did not expect.

Many university students live like the younger son in this parable, spending their time, energy, and (often their parents') money on the fleeting pleasures of this world. Many eagerly leave home to live the life of freedom they have long dreamed of. They depart, have the time of their life, but often return to their rooms at night strangely homesick. In my experience as a university ministry worker, these students are not homesick for a place but a person. College students want Jesus; many just don't know it yet! Like all human beings, they want the assurance of acceptance and the intimacy that accompanies belonging. They want to be fully known and fully loved. They want a sense of peace for their restless souls.

Today, the true Father is calling many university students to himself. He kindly opens their eyes to see the darkness of their sin and the light of his love. What greater privilege is there than to see students come to "proclaim the excellencies of him who called [them] out of darkness into his marvelous light" (1 Pet. 2:9)? Each time we share the gospel with students, friends, coworkers, or family members, we are giving them a chance to finally come home. We are giving them the chance to have, in full, what their hearts already long for: forgiveness, true intimacy, and shalom.

THE BEAUTY OF THE CAMPUS

I became a Christian my first year of college. In the context of a messy romantic breakup and the stresses of being a collegiate athlete, I became curious about the God I'd heard about growing up. I began reading the New Testament in January of my first year, and two things became clear, drawing me to trust in Christ as my Savior: my sin offended God, and Christ offered forgiveness. Shortly after coming to faith, I became involved with the university ministry with which I now serve as a staff member. Having spent ten years with university students, I am convinced that the context of higher education is one of the most strategic and effective contexts in which to share the gospel and to disciple others.

Let's be honest: college is pretty much the only time in life when you interact regularly and often live with your best friends, who are just about all in the same season of life and age as yourself. You eat, play, work, and hang out with these friends. The college years can be some of the most formative: so much of who a person will be in adulthood is shaped, formed, and molded during this short time. University students have more flexible time than they will perhaps ever again have in their life (although many of my students will object to that point). They have availability and energy to be discipled and to share the gospel in ways that post-college life often does not afford, with its growing responsibilities of job and family. Students will give their energy during these years of higher education as they are being shaped and formed to have an impact on the world. They are our future doctors, teachers, lawyers, mothers, fathers, pastors, deacons, etc. There are wonderfully brilliant and diverse men and women attending the various educational institutions in our world today. My heart longs that they would see and know Jesus before they move on.

Although college students are generally in the same age bracket, every student on a campus has a unique story, and distinctive desires and aspirations. They come into college with a broad spectrum of spiritual interests and backgrounds. That being said, in an effort to learn the demographic I am sharing my faith with, I have noticed trends in the types of students I engage. There are four types of students I consistently meet on the campus where I serve:

- The Interested—students eager to grow in their walk with God and to share their faith.
- The Uninterested—students with little to no interest in God, the Bible, or anything pertaining to Christianity.
- The Curious—students who are unbelievers searching for "something more" in life.
- The Churched—students who come into college with deep exposure to Christianity but with a spiritual boredom and sleepiness.

THE INTERESTED

Although it feels like more and more of a rarity these days, some students step onto the university campus excited and eager to grow in their walk with the Lord. Perhaps they grew up in a godly Christian home or became a Christian in high school through their youth ministry or a faithful friend sharing the gospel with them. Maybe they cannot remember a day in their life when they did not love the Lord. Perhaps they were even discipled through a faithful youth ministry leader. Whatever their story, these believing students are often looking to get connected to a group of believers who are eager to grow in the Lord as well. Furthermore, for college ministry staff workers working predominantly among non-Christians, they are usually a breath of fresh air.

I met Emily her freshman year.[2] She was very involved with youth ministry in high school and was excited about growing spiritually during her time in college and sharing the gospel with her teammates. Possessing much zeal and little tact, Emily often reminded me of the apostle Peter in the Gospels (and myself as a college student). I was thankful for this. I will take zeal over tact any day! Tact can be taught with time and maturity; zeal, excitement, and a fervent spirit are evidences of God's grace in a person's life. She was not afraid to stand up for the name of the Lord, no matter the social cost.

Because Emily came into college already a Christian, my influence in her life was through discipleship rather than evangelism. We spent much of our time together talking about the fundamentals of the Christian faith: knowing God through studying his Word, experiencing intimacy with God through prayer, being used by the Holy Spirit in relational evangelism, and experiencing the joy of Christ in biblical community (namely, the local church).

When we study the Gospels, it is evident that Jesus was with his disciples often. Whether he was praying (Luke 9:18), teaching (Matt. 5:1), or performing miracles (John 2:2), the disciples were not far away from him. They saw his life "up close and personal." Whether they were witnessing the most spectacular event their eyes would ever see (such as the transfiguration in Matthew 17), or an incredibly vulnerable moment when Jesus identified with the sting of death (such as at the death of Lazarus in John 11), they witnessed the Master in a variety of contexts and a plethora of emotions (sadness, anger, grief, joy, etc.).

My relationship with Emily confirmed this invaluable lesson about discipleship: never go alone. When I was meeting with first-year girls in the dorms and sharing my faith, Emily was often by my side. I tried to expose her to as much of my life as possible, which is both humbling and terrifying. It was important that she be exposed to the ministry portion of my life and also the everyday tasks, such as grocery shopping, running errands, etc. We learned together what it meant to "preach the word; be ready in season and out of season" (2 Tim. 4:2); you never know when an ordinary trip to the grocery store can be used for redemptive purposes.

Other students came to college completely uninterested in the things of God, such as Emily's close friend and teammate Alexis, for whom we were consistently praying. We asked God to penetrate Alexis's heart. The beauty of God's call on our lives is that he often saves those among the uninterested.

THE UNINTERESTED

Alexis stepped onto the college campus possessing a heart of stone. I mean that spiritually and metaphorically. Alexis exuded a tough exterior, and unlike Emily, she had not grown up in a family or a context that knew Jesus. She had no interest in knowing about the God of the Bible.

When I first met Alexis, I knocked on the door of her freshman dorm to tell her she had won a prize from the raffle that we did for first-year students (we have done a raffle every year as a way to gauge spiritual interest, build relationships, and talk to students about the gospel). When she answered the door, I remember she looked tired, stressed, and rigid. We engaged in small talk and chatted about our mutual connection with Emily. But we shortly found ourselves in a spiritual conversation as I asked her what her thoughts were on spiritual things: "Did you grow up going to church?" "Do you believe there is a God?" "What do you believe about God?" She made it clear—in a direct way, I might add—that she was not interested in Christianity or the Lord. I walked away thinking that I would probably never see or talk to her again. *Maybe God is just not at work in her life*, I thought to myself.

But Emily was praying for Alexis. I am ashamed to admit that Alexis felt like a lost cause to me, and I thought I was right until the end of the spring semester that year. As the Lord gave opportunity, Emily continued to share her faith with Alexis throughout the school year—and, when she invited Alexis to church, Alexis came. It was one evening at church that Alexis heard the gospel again (for the twentieth time, it felt like), and she believed it for the first time. We went back to their campus, and Emily and I shared the gospel again with Alexis, who received it gladly. She put her faith in Christ the Son of God who took the punishment for her sins on the cross, who rose from the dead, and who lives even now in heaven. Together we prayed and thanked God for taking out her heart of stone and replacing it with a heart of flesh (Ezek. 36:26).

Emily reminded me of the command to be persistent in prayer (Col. 4:2). God reminded me that we do not have the power or foreknowledge to know whom God is calling to himself. Furthermore, his arm is not too short to save. Alexis's tough exterior and hostile initial interaction led me to believe that God was not working in her life. But the Holy Spirit is often moving in people in ways we cannot see. After she came to faith, I discipled Alexis for the remainder of her time in college. The Lord used her mightily on the campus to share her faith and disciple other students. We are still good friends today, and she is still sharing the gospel.

God saves the uninterested. We need not steer clear or be afraid of those who initially stiff-arm us in opposition. Our greatest biblical example of this is none other than the apostle Paul. Alexis was like Paul in that regard: initially uninterested and even hostile, but then redeemed and used by God as a chosen instrument to take the gospel to other uninterested people (Acts 9:15). If you have been sharing the gospel and praying for years for a student, a family member, or a friend, take heart that God is often working in ways we may not be able to see. "Do not be slothful in zeal, be fervent in spirit, serve the Lord" (Rom. 12:11). As long as they are living, there is hope that the uninterested can "come home."

THE CURIOUS

Spiritually curious students are like my five-year-old nephew, who prefers to slowly dip his toes in the pool water in order to test the temperature. (Personally, I prefer the total immersion method.) These students are poking around, trying to find truth. That's where Kelly was when I met her in her dorm room.

Kelly came from a tough home. An emotionally absent father and various personal struggles left her walking into her first year of university with a metaphorical limp. The hardship of life left her tired and cynical, but a part of her remained hopeful that there was some higher power that cared.

I remember telling Kelly there was a way she could know truth, and I asked her to read God's Word with me once a week for thirty minutes. As I write this, I can remember my heart rate increasing as I fumbled over the question. Her excited response surprised me. With little to no spiritual background, Kelly was eager and excited. Furthermore, with little to no knowledge of Jesus, she drank in every word of Scripture with excitement.

Sharing the gospel with Kelly was such a joy! Everything was so new and exciting that her joy of becoming acquainted with Jesus rubbed off on me as well. We started studying the Gospel of John once a week. It did not take long for Kelly to realize that God's Word, a book she had never read, knew more about her spiritual condition than anyone else, including herself. Like all of us, Kelly began to see that she "loved the darkness rather than the light" (John 3:19). She began to see that her deepest need, to be brought into a relationship with God, was fulfilled in Jesus's atoning work on the cross.

I remember the day we both marveled at John 1:14: "And the Word became flesh and dwelt among us, and we have seen his glory, the glory as of the only Son from the Father, full of grace and truth."

"So God became a human? Like, he used the bathroom and stuff?"

"Yeah, that among other things," I chuckled.

We discussed how crazy it was that the God of Genesis 1 who had the power to speak everything into existence, brought himself so low that he became like one of us to save us. God actually identified with us on the deepest level possible—as a human! Jesus experienced everything that we experienced, yet was without sin (Heb. 4:15). We do not serve an aloof God, but one who sees, hears, and understands our greatest joys and the deepest sorrows. In my relationship with Kelly, God taught me to fight to hold on to my wonder.

God also reminded me that his Word is sufficient to save. Our fancy methods and catchy questions and sayings can be helpful, but the living and active Word of God is what grips people's hearts and exposes them to truth as the Holy Spirit draws them. While not everyone may have the opportunity to sit down with a person and study God's Word weekly, people can hear God's Word through his people who store it up in their hearts (Ps. 119:11). The Bible is our greatest asset in sharing the gospel. We can let it do the heavy lifting in our evangelistic relationships.

THE CHURCHED

The churched student (again, not all, but some) comes into college with a significant problem: she believes that what she does and what she knows are sufficient for her salvation.

Many who have grown up in the church can get so used to hearing about the beauty of the Lord that their hearts harden against the gospel. In some cases the gospel may have been clearly preached and their ears simply were not open. The news that is meant to cause rejoicing results in boredom. The churched student is full of Bible knowledge, yet all the while she is starving for a relationship with Jesus. This was who I was my first year in college.

For as long as I can remember, I grew up sitting in a church pew. I have fond memories of the elaborate church hats women would wear, the vibrant beat of the songs, and the older women who fed me peppermints. I knew the songs, the Scripture, the right answers, but my heart was unengaged and uninterested. I spent the first eighteen years of my life trying to earn God's favor. Like many women, I was fighting to be perfect. As a result, I thought I could earn God's approval the way I earned man's: sheer grit, hard work, being nice, and doing good deeds. But my legalistic lifestyle did not lead to the joy I was seeking.

My "try harder" and "do better" mentality often left me feeling spiritually frustrated and emotionally tired. I knew that even with all the "spiritual accolades" and biblical information I acquired, my reach for perfection fell undeniably short (Rom. 3:23). I entered college with the false assumption that biblical knowledge equaled an intimate relationship with God, but actually I was desperately lost. I needed to be called to repentance and faith in Jesus Christ—and to the never-ending wonder of being reconciled to God by a Savior who loves and cares for me.

I meet many students who resemble my eighteen-year-old self. Perhaps this is the scariest place to be: under a false assurance of salvation based on works and knowledge. Students such as these have "figured out" God as one figures out a math problem and moves on. This know-it-all mentality leaves one with little humility for God's inexhaustible nature. Instead of being a loving Father, he becomes a cosmic genie one calls on when we want something. An inexhaustible God gets reduced to mere facts on a page.

When after college I moved to Lynchburg, Virginia, I experienced deep joy in finding the newest traffic shortcuts, hole-in-the-wall restaurants, and "secret spots" that the city had to offer. Almost seven years later, the discovery of such places never ends, and each new finding brings a new element of joy and wonder. Similarly, through my own spiritual story and through those around me, God continues to teach me that part of the beauty of the gospel is found in constantly seeing and discovering new elements of it. There is little room for boredom when it comes to our relationship with Jesus as we dig ever deeper into his Word. As we run the race set before us with endurance, we have a chance to marvel at the great salvation God reveals to us along the way. There is immense joy in the discovery, even as we know Christ better and better.

DIFFERENT SOILS

I wish I could say that everyone I have shared the gospel with has responded in faith and has gone on to walk with the Lord. As much joy as God has brought through ministering to college students, there has also been deep sorrow as I have watched some students I thought loved the Lord walk away from the faith.

One girl I shared the gospel with professed faith in Christ, and I began to disciple her—only to see her walk away from the faith three years later. She currently has little to no interest in Jesus. Another girl I invested in now rejects altogether the very notion of a knowable God. Both are now steeped in patterns of sexual sin. There is undoubtedly a sense of heartache that accompanies watching women you thought knew the Lord turn away to other gods.

"Was it me?" "Is there something I could have done?" "But

she was showing personal fruit in her life." As I have turned things over in my mind, these are only a few of the questions that have circulated during restless nights. I did not know what I expected in my evangelistic efforts, but it was not that.

God gives us a glimpse of what we can expect as we are faithful to share the good news of the gospel. People will invariably respond to the Word of God in different ways. For some, the gospel will take root, grip their hearts, and bring them to their knees in repentance and lasting fruit. Sadly, for others, God's Word will come and go like the passing of the wind.

In the account of the parable of the sower (Matt. 13:18–23; Mark 4:1–20; Luke 8:4–15), seeds are sown on the path, on the rocks, among thorns, and in good soil. The seed pictures the Word of God, and the soils represent different responses to God's Word. For one person, the Word is like seed sown on a path: the Devil snatches it away so that she does not believe. For another, the Word is like seed sown on the rocks: she hears the Word and receives it with joy, but she has no root and so falls away in times of trials. For a third, the Word is like seed sown among thorns: this one hears the Word, but the lure of the world and what it has to offer choke the Word, and there is no fruit. But for the final person, the Word is like seed sown in good soil: she hears the Word, believes it, holds fast to it, and bears fruit. We can expect that some seeds will flourish into beautiful evidences of God's grace, and others may not.

In Luke's account of the seed sown on good soil, he speaks of "those who, hearing the word, hold it fast in an honest and good heart and *bear fruit with patience*" (Luke 8:15). The seeds that do bear fruit do so *with patience*. The fruit bearing is slow, tedious, and sometimes unnoticeable, but it is there. Another translation reads, "Having heard the word with an honest and good heart, hold on to it and by enduring, bear fruit" (Luke 8:15 CSB). Our endurance sets us apart as true believers in the Lord Jesus. I am not sure which kind of soil best pictures the lives of those two girls I thought had come to know the Lord; however, I do know the faith they had was not an enduring one. The seed of God's Word had not fallen on good soil.

DO NOT GROW WEARY OF DOING GOOD

Regardless of where you find yourself laboring to make Jesus's name famous, it is likely to be long and hard work. Perhaps that is why Paul called it labor and toil (1 Cor. 15:58; Col. 1:29; 1 Tim. 4:10). College ministry is no different. If I am honest, there have been times I am tempted to quit because the work seems too hard, almost impossible. And it *is* impossible; we have an impossible job. We cannot make spiritually dead people come to life. But we know the one who can. We know that God supernaturally uses our efforts to do just that. He commands us to "not grow weary of doing good" (Gal. 6:9) in part because we are commonly tempted to do so. But if we endure, we are likely to see a few new births, a few resurrections. And those will multiply.

Even when it is hard, we must never give up. The hope of the resurrection promises that our labor is not in vain. "Therefore, my beloved brothers, be steadfast, immovable, always abounding in the work of the Lord, knowing that in the Lord your labor is not in vain" (1 Cor. 15:58). As we "abound in the work of the Lord" for God's glory, he will use us as agents of change. And as God uses us as agents of change, he also changes us, his workmanship, created in Christ Jesus for good works.

My days as a college minister are unimpressive. As I go about each day, which is often filled with doing the same small and faithful tasks, I pray that I would continue in the good works God has prepared beforehand for me to walk in (Eph. 2:10). Mine is slow, steady plodding day in and day out, intermingled with much prayer, sharing the gospel, and trusting that students will respond. Through these labors, amazingly, God redeems. He brings his children home to himself.

8

Spreading the Word in the Workplace

Happy Khambule

with Kathleen Nielson

In response to this topic "Evangelism in the Workplace," the stereotype that might come to mind is that of a person who is constantly explaining a quick outline of how to be saved to each and every person in her work environment. It is certainly true that to *evangelize* is "to herald or proclaim the good news of Jesus Christ." And yet, a person with an evangelist's heart is not necessarily a full-time preacher offering to everyone in her path a "one-size-fits-all" message. As Christians, we evangelize by living evangelistic lives—lives that will include sharing the Word of God and the Savior that Word reveals.

EVANGELISM GROWS OUT OF THE CHURCH

Jesus told the disciples to follow him and he would make them fishers of men (Mark 1:17), and then he sent them out two by two to preach to people to repent, turn from their sinful ways, and put their faith and trust in Jesus Christ. When we follow Jesus, we become part of his disciples, his body—his church. And in that church we learn about the gospel so that we can live it and share it with others, letting them know the good news about God and his redemptive plan for all peoples. As disciples, we are called to grow and multiply; the good news is given to us as the talents were given to those servants in Jesus's parable (Matt. 25:14–30). Consider: every time you hear the Word of God preached in your local church, you are given a coin, a talent, which God calls you to multiply according to your ability. We are responsible and accountable to God for what he has given us.

Evangelism in the workplace is the outcome and extension of the preaching and ministry from the local church. By God's grace, my experience has been that of being equipped in my church congregation for witness in various spheres of life outside of that congregation. This equipping happens through pastors and elders who regularly preach and teach God's Word, and through lay men and women who teach and model that Word among the body of Christ in all kinds of ways. The gospel among believers is not something that happened to us long ago; it is the constant focus of God's Word taught and the reason for our joy and hope: we believers are those whom God has redeemed and whom he empowers through the Spirit of the risen Christ in us.

God places us in particular professions and callings so as to be his witnesses, spread like salt and light in the world. We take in the Word of God regularly among God's people, learning to understand and apply it in our Christian walk—and we carry that Word with us as we walk! We hear and trust the promise Jesus first gave to his disciples following his resurrection:

> But you will receive power when the Holy Spirit has come upon you, and you will be my witnesses in Jerusalem and in all Judea and Samaria, and to the end of the earth. (Acts 1:8)

EVANGELISM: BEING AND SHARING GOOD NEWS

Evangelism grows out of the regular patterns of our lives. As witnesses of Christ, we understand that evangelism in a working environment can happen because that is where we often spend at least eight to ten hours per day. We share life with the people around us during those hours—and they must see the gospel at work in our lives. We must *be* good news as we *share* the good news. The apostle Paul puts it this way, writing to the people in Thessalonica with whom he had shared the gospel:

> We were gentle among you, like a nursing mother taking care of her own children. So, being affectionately desirous of you, we were ready to share with you not only the gospel of God but also our own selves, because you had become very dear to us. (1 Thess. 2:7–8)

Paul is clear: we must communicate the gospel not only with words but also by showing love and care for others. Such a combination results in an open door to share more about our faith in Christ.

In my own workplace, I've learned the power of combining love and words. I work at a hospital in Dubai, in the United Arab Emirates, as a perfusionist in open-heart surgery. A perfusionist manages the heart-lung machine that takes over the function of the heart and lungs during open-heart surgery. Basically, the life of a patient is in my hands as the cardiac surgeon is operating. The anesthesiologist will switch off his ventilator when I start my machine.

When patients and their relatives come to a hospital for surgery, they are anxious and worried about the outcome of the procedure. They give their lives into the hands of the surgical team and the postoperative intensive care department. As a Christian in this environment, how then should I work as an ambassador of Christ? As a perfusionist in this context, I am constantly reminded that I do not work for an earthly king but for King Jesus. Here are a few questions I regularly ask:

- Does my behavior reflect Christ in my integrity and in the care and quality of my work?
- How are my relationships with my manager, colleagues, and customers or patients?
- What is my reaction if and when I am misjudged or passed over for a promotion?
- Is my speech controlled, positive, kind, and truthful? And am I ready to speak of Christ?

In Colossians 3:17, 22–24, the apostle Paul addresses such matters, calling all believers to live and act as representatives of the Lord Jesus—and as bondservants in particular who do their work not just to please people but ultimately to please our Lord Jesus:

> And whatever you do, in word or deed, do everything in the name of the Lord Jesus, giving thanks to God the Father through him. . . . Bondservants, obey in everything those who are your earthly masters, not by way of eye-service, as people-pleasers, but with sincerity of heart, fearing the Lord. Whatever you do, work heartily, as for the Lord and not for men, knowing that from the Lord you will receive the inheritance as your reward. You are serving the Lord Christ.

In so serving the Lord Christ, we reflect him to those around us, drawing others to him. We show his goodness, often without words, by who we are and what we do. Those in the medical profession care for human beings who were created by God in his image. We show forth God's image, even as we care for his creation, by caring for the bodies he made. And, of course, we show his goodness in the way we relate to everyone around us, especially in the words we speak.

GLIMPSES OF EVANGELISM AT WORK

For two years, I have been spending my hospital tea and lunch breaks with Christabel, a fellow South African also working in

Dubai. As I came to know Christabel, to chat with her and eat with her, it was natural to talk with her about the Scripture passages I regularly prepared for discussion in my church's Tuesday community Bible study group. I explained how we do the Bible study: we observe the context of the passage and look for the author's intent to the original reading audience and to us today, we aim to find the main ideas, and we discuss ways we can apply what we have learned.

When I told Christabel that in every part of Scripture we need to highlight the gospel of God's grace to us in Jesus Christ, that prompted a question: "What is the gospel, Happy?" I helped my friend to understand the biblical truths about God our Creator; human beings who have turned away from God; Jesus, who through his death and resurrection reconciles us to God; and our response of faith. As my friend listened carefully, God softened her heart, and she was interested to join us in our community Bible study to learn more. Sharing the gospel at work often leads into shared connections outside of work, especially through the church.

In our church Bible study, we always alert each other about the religious background of visitors so that we can be sensitive not to chase them away from hearing about Jesus. Christabel was from a Catholic background, and we took care to speak of that background with respect. We saw that Christabel had never been taught the Bible; we also quickly saw that she loved learning and taking it to heart—she was hungry and ready. The Word does the work; and as the Spirit works, we are there to help! Christabel got connected and attended our group weekly, always bringing her nicely organized folder, including the entire Bible study prepared for that session and the materials to be discussed. She began to come every Friday to attend our church service. Our lunchtime at work together became more intentional as we worked through the study, helping each other along. We still spend time together at lunchtime, sharing the Word of God.

Christabel's daughter visited her in Dubai for two months, and I invited her to come with us to church. She was stunned to hear how the Word of God is preached, and she loved hearing the way our pastor made the point of the sermon the point of the Scripture passage from which he spoke. As she listened, the Spirit exposed the sin in her heart, and she understood how much we are all in need of Jesus Christ, who died on the cross for our sins. She was hungry to know more and wanted us to spend more time together talking about the gospel. She visited our women's Bible study where we were discussing the book of Galatians, in which Paul explains that there is only one gospel through which we are justified:

> Yet we know that a person is not justified by works of the law but through faith in Jesus Christ, so we also have believed in Christ Jesus, in order to be justified by faith in Christ and not by works of the law, because by works of the law no one will be justified. (Gal. 2:16)

Just like Christabel, her daughter was hungry for the truth. She would come to my place often to talk about what it means to believe the gospel and to walk with God. One night, as I was having dinner with Christabel and her daughter, her daughter explained to her mother that she now clearly understood and believed the gospel. She explained that as she returned to South Africa, she wanted to look for a church that taught the Bible—"Because, Mom, now I know the truth and I want to grow more in the Lord." She had come to Dubai at a time in her life when she felt hopeless, and now the hopelessness in her life was healed as she received God's grace in Christ and came to rejoice in her salvation through the death and resurrection of Jesus. She is now connected to a gospel-centered church.

Through God's grace to me in sending Christabel and her daughter my way, I learned even more clearly that God is the one who prepares the hearts of people for his Word to be planted. As we water and nurture, God will make the seed of his Word to grow as he sees fit. Sometimes we see the fruit; sometimes we do not. Our part is to be faithful in living and sharing the gospel truth of Jesus Christ. It might all start over tea or coffee during a break at work!

And it might take a long time, sometimes years. One nurse at the hospital became my friend—another woman from South Africa. She did not know Christ as her personal Savior. She knew I was a Christian, and my constant involvement in church activities used to puzzle her: Why did I have to attend church so often, and then also attend midweek Bible studies, and then also meet with various ladies one on one to talk about our faith? This friend would laugh and say, "My friend, God will be angry that you call him every day!" I started sharing the Word of God with this woman when opportunities arose; the good thing was that she was not at all resistant to listen. But whenever I would invite her to come with me to church, she would say, "No, my friend, next time in the near future." But she was searching. There were times when she would come to my office and say, "My friend, I am not all right today. Can you read something in the Bible and pray for me?" I thanked God for those opportunities and continued to pray for her. Eventually, this woman finished her contract and went back home to South Africa.

After about three years, she sent me this email:

Hi my friend,

Having known you has opened my eyes about the Word of God. I remember going to church but not understanding what the fuss was all about. . . . Through you, my friend, I started reading my Bible to understand the Word of God. There was a day I asked you how does one fast, and you sat me down to explain in detail with Bible verses that went with fasting. . . . I started to understand how God works through his servants. . . . I remember you telling me to pray for my family. . . . When I came back to South Africa, I started going to church every Sunday until I accepted Jesus as my Savior, and I have never looked back! Today I can attest that you played a role in my life with the Lord. Today I make sure I wake up every morning to pray and read my Bible the way you taught me to observe, find meaning, and apply it—my life is not the same. . . . God is now in every decision I make, this is through your teachings, my friend. I always reflect back to how you used to carry yourself as a Christian. . . . I thank God for you, my friend.[1]

REALIZING OUR ROLE IN EVANGELISM

Jesus said, "I am the light of the world. Whoever follows me will not walk in darkness, but will have the light of life" (John 8:12). My nurse friend needed someone to share that light and call her to open her eyes to the gospel truth of Jesus Christ. I am thinking about a lighthouse that has a bright light called a *beacon*, used by sailors at night to help them guide the ship. This light serves as a navigation aid for the maritime pilots to avoid dangers along the coastline. They are able to gauge the distance to avoid shipwreck on rocks off the seashore and enter the harbor safely. We Christians should be lighthouses to the dying world, shining the light of Christ to those who don't know that the wages of sin is death. It is a privilege to share with them that they can be spared the wrath of God by turning to Christ, who bore that wrath for us on the cross.

As people of God in the workplace, we must have as our goal to be employees who demonstrate the gospel and through whom people are drawn to Christ. In my hospital, we have an "Employee of the Month" recognition in which a staff member is selected based on written appraisals from other staff, patients, and families. The appraisal is based on the "Six Values of Service Excellence" that the hospital celebrates. Of course, one of those values is attention to excellence in our work. And one of those values is compassion: we employees are taught how we can demonstrate empathy, show kindness to patients and families, anticipate patients' needs, and meet those needs with excellence and care. As staff, we are to adhere to these values and behavior when dealing with every person coming to our hospital. What a great call for a Christian, who recognizes these values as ways of living out the love of God our Creator and the love of Christ our Redeemer. This kind of compassion, for example, must be our aim not only in a hospital environment but also in all places of work.

Once we had a patient who was very sick and came to our hospital for heart surgery. His family was extremely anxious and restless. I always speak to families and patients, encouraging them to have hope. When it is possible, I ask if I can pray with them, and I ask them to pray that God will give us wisdom during the operation. I was able to do so in this case. The surgery went well, and I went to see the patient and the family in the intensive care unit every day during his recovery. I gave them regular support and encouraged them to put their faith and trust in God. The next month I was recognized as Employee of the Month; here is the message written on the Service Excellence card:

> Ms. Happy was a great support to us from the time we came to the hospital, during surgery and post-surgery. We appreciate the professional way she handled our case. It was a delight to have her support. She showed godly compassion and her smile was a constant comfort to us. We wish her the best in her life and career.

In fact, without offering further details I can testify that God has changed their lives; they now testify about the wonderful Comforter and Savior Christ Jesus.

I tell these stories to give glory only to God. He is the one who saves. Let us work as unto the Lord whether we are recognized or not, knowing that our reward is in heaven. We are called to follow Jesus, who during his earthly ministry showed compassion to the harassed, hurting, and helpless because he saw them as sheep without a shepherd (Matt. 9:36). We are placed in our jobs to be the instruments in God's hand, working so that many will see and turn to Christ, who is the Good Shepherd so desperately needed by the harassed and hurting people all around us.

REJOICING IN GROWING GLIMPSES OF EVANGELISM

I've been encouraged in my efforts to share the gospel by the stories of many others; we need to hear these stories! We believers need to share them with one another. In my interactions especially with other women in my church, it has made a difference to hear many tell about how they spend their break times in their workplaces, giving themselves to others—and how God uses these small efforts. These conversations have made me more ready to be likewise a good ambassador of Christ, confident that I am where God has placed me for his good purposes. We need the encouragement and prayers of fellow believers.

I recall a discussion panel during a conference on faith and work at our church. It was so helpful to hear the stories told by panel members as they acknowledged successes and failures, boldness and fear. One woman's account was especially encouraging as she answered the question: "How have you thought about being a Christian witness in the workplace?" I was happy to see that, right at the start, she had the mind-set of one who is intentional and passionate about taking the gospel into the workplace. This is what she shared with us:

> I would try to find a way to let people at my workplace know as soon as possible that I am a Christian. The longer you go without saying it or modeling it, the more awkward you will feel and the harder it will be to do later. I had the opportunity to do so in my interview, when my colleagues asked why I moved to Dubai. I told them that I was a Christian, and we wanted to move somewhere in the Middle East, but we wanted to be in a city that had a faithful, gospel-preaching church. We knew Dubai had two great churches, so my husband applied

for jobs here. It helped that I could naturally and immediately share that with them, so that it's been easier for me to talk about my faith in the months following. It's not always easy, but I'm praying for boldness to persevere and fear nothing, but to share the gospel.

This woman had listened well to God's Word spoken through the apostle Peter:

> Now who is there to harm you if you are zealous for what is good? But even if you should suffer for righteousness' sake, you will be blessed. Have no fear of them, nor be troubled, but in your hearts honor Christ the Lord as holy, always being prepared to make a defense to anyone who asks you for a reason for the hope that is in you; yet do it with gentleness and respect, having a good conscience, so that, when you are slandered, those who revile your good behavior in Christ may be put to shame. For it is better to suffer for doing good, if that should be God's will, than for doing evil. (1 Pet. 3:13–17)

Many here in Dubai work in companies where there might be reason to fear sharing the gospel; this is the Middle East, full of different nationalities and religious backgrounds. But we must not fear to share our faith. Of course, you can start a conversation just by asking a friend how they spent their weekend. That will open a door and perhaps bring questions as you tell them about your weekend. And maybe that will lead to a shared cup of tea or coffee.

A FINAL ENCOURAGEMENT TO SHARE THE WORD

I enjoy hearing the stories of fellow church members and how they came to faith. When we have a baptismal service, it is especially meaningful to hear those being baptized give their testimonies of how God drew them and saved them. Such testimonies lift our eyes to the God who saves. One faithful church member named Lynn shared a bit about seeing God draw people in her workplace. This is her story:

> I can't tell you how many times I asked the Lord for opportunities to share the gospel with my colleagues. Each time my husband and other friends in full-time ministry shared, my heart both leapt and hurt. How wonderful to hear how lives were being changed! If only I had that kind of time. If only my situation was different. If only people around me showed such interest. If only.
>
> It isn't that my workplace was void of opportunities. When I made an effort to leave my area of work on breaks and get out listening to others, I had the chance to invest in people. Sometimes it was reading a Christian book together one on one. Sometimes it was praying for someone. At times I had significant gospel conversations. However, it was often sporadic and inconsistent, producing little visible fruit.
>
> "We are seeing lives changed by just getting people in the Word and letting God speak to them," my husband would share. I felt that he and the others were so fortunate to be able to lead studies that were most often done in a manuscript style: students would gather around with the portion of the Bible printed out and would spend hours poring over the text together.
>
> I longed to study the Bible with my colleagues, knowing that his Word is what changes lives. "What do you think about starting a Bible study during lunchtime? I don't know what it will look like, and it might only be three people, but let's just do it," I asked one of the few Christians in my workplace. I'm embarrassed that it took so long to come to that point.
>
> All the "if onlys," mixed with the busyness of the job and my sin, were laid at the foot at the cross. And the Word began to do the work that I so longed for! It no longer had to be me devising the right words to say or searching for opportunities. We set a time, one a day a week during our lunch break, and invited everyone to come. We simply read the Bible together

over lunch—not a study, no homework, and no manuscript layout. We read the Scripture as we munched our food. With the Word projected on a screen, we read. We spent two years in the Gospel of Mark and another year in Romans. God brought my colleagues. We read the Word; we talked about it, and as God tells us in Isaiah 55:11: "So shall my word be that goes out from my mouth; it shall not return to me empty, but it shall accomplish that which I purpose, and shall succeed in the thing for which I sent it."

Soon, all the opportunities that I longed for were there! The gospel was so clear every week. Not through my words but through the very Word of God. Those who knew the Lord already were encouraged, challenged, and began reaching out to others at work. Those who did not yet believe—some from other faith backgrounds—heard the gospel and, by God's grace, came again and again. Relationships deepened and interest developed. Some got involved in healthy churches. Some began reading their Bibles on their own at home. This happened working full-time within a secular workplace on our lunch break. God was true to his Word, and it has not returned empty.

God is true to his Word. It will not return empty. His Word lights up the gospel given to us in the Lord Jesus; our privilege is to share this gospel until Jesus comes again. May we all have more and more stories to tell about how God uses us in the places where he puts us, to share this good news with many—for Christ's glory alone.

9

Spreading the Word among Friends Identifying as LGBTQ

Rosaria Butterfield

A STORY ABOUT MY NEIGHBOR

It was a surprise visit from an old friend, someone who was like an aunt to my children and a sister to me.[1] The running and jumping and squeals of delight belted out like a Broadway musical. They shook the house.

"Miss Maisie is HERE! Did you hear me, Mom? MISS MAISIE! SHE'S BACK!"

Maisie walked through the door to the kitchen, and just like old times, the kids were all over her, the dogs were doing flips with joy, and I felt a love for this old friend that traveled deep and wide, back into the caverns of my past.

Maisie was the neighbor who marched down the street with a plate of homemade brownies, donning Doc Martens and a butch haircut, familiar throwbacks to my former life as a lesbian. I was a newly married Christian woman with a secret lesbian past. In our new life in Virginia, only my husband, Kent, knew my past.

Maisie both terrified and comforted me, all at the same time.

She and Kent became fast friends and early-morning walking partners.

Kent and I started to adopt children out of foster care. Maisie and Mary Jo started to adopt children out of foster care. Soon, we were the two transracial families on the block. Our children loved to play together. We shared values about electronics. But our relationship was set in stone forever when one day my son rode his bike on the street in front of our houses without his helmet. Maisie saw this infraction. She told Michael to go and put on his helmet. When he refused, she took his bike away. For a week. It was pure joy to live down the block from grown-ups.

Maisie was the best. Our children grew up together, and so did we. Our friendship survived the shock waves of a culture war that makes casualties out of friendships like ours.

One summer while the kids were still little, Maisie and I spent long hours on her porch talking about faith and sexuality, about Jesus and suffering. Our children played in the dirt with shovels, and then in the garden, where Maisie had set up painting play stations with paint and brushes, easels and canvases. After awhile, the children started carrying chickens and baby goats to and fro, leaving paint-dipped finger tips on their feathers and fur. Maisie was a walking Montessori experience, and my children could not get enough of her.

Ours was a complex and wonderful friendship.

My children have known that I was a lesbian from their earliest memory. It would come up in family devotions. They cut their teeth on the new words and alphabet-identities that circle around us today. They had to. They have me for a mother.

My children have always known that conversion to Christ meant that I had to give up things I loved and people I loved.

My children knew that Maisie and Mary Jo were just like Mama used to be.

Sin understood in the landscape of God's saving grace.

In the years that Maisie and Mary Jo and their kids lived down the block, a lot happened. These were politically charged days. DOMA—the Defense of Marriage Act defining marriage as the union of one man and one woman—came up (1996) and then down (2013). When Obergefell finally reigned supreme (2015), granting the LGBTQ community the right to marry in the United States, all hell broke loose on the local and national scene regarding LGBTQ rights.

In spite of this, our two households remained friends.

Maisie and I, though, were special friends. Friends who could talk about heart things—broken hearts especially.

Maisie and Mary Jo had been together for two decades. They slept in two separate parts of the house. They had stopped having sex at about the time the children started coming. Had I high-horsed into the kitchen with Bible in hand, accusing Maisie of sexual sin, she would have laughed me out the door. No, the sin in that house wasn't sexual, even though both women identified as lesbian, had gotten legally married in Canada, and were looking forward to renewing their vows in the United States after Obergefell made this a reality. The sin went deeper than that. The sin was unbelief.

Mary Jo was the breadwinner and Maisie the stay-at-home mom. Mary Jo was a heart surgeon. Her work life was crazy-intense, and without the kind company of the Holy Spirit to call us to repentance and change, we all simply do the best we can in the wisdom of the flesh that we have. Soon the arguments between them grew with their distance. Maisie would cry softly as she recounted last night's fight, ashamed that the children could hear all of this. We talked, warm mugs of tea in hand, and the "Love Makes a Family" poster in her kitchen seemed to mock at every fallen tear.

In spite of the pain in that relationship, Maisie had no intention of leaving, and Mary Jo had no intention of asking her to leave. Their sexual passion had morphed to political solidarity and a deep loyalty that it's hard to explain outside of lesbian relationships. It was a deeply codependent sense of ownership that they each exercised over the other. Love that is not mediated by Christ can eat you alive. Mary Jo and Maisie were a family of choice and planned to stay that way, come hell or high water.

In spite of our differences, they trusted my husband and me with precious things.

When "marriage equality" came up, they wanted to know why we opposed such basic rights.

"Maisie," I said, "God doesn't want me to put a stumbling block between you and the God who made you."

"That's a pile of crap," she said as she stormed out of my kitchen.

They trusted us with their children. Their oldest daughter, Tiffy, could have been my twin at twenty. Tiff loved literature and Latin. When she left for college, my children grieved. When she returned, Tiff spent long hours at my dining room table as we would pore over Goethe and Cicero together. During summer vacations and spring break, she was my children's favorite babysitter and reading tutor.

They trusted us with their problems. Like most members of the LGBTQ community, they felt deeply the needs of the marginalized. They cared for the poor and the homeless and the infirm.

My aged Mom who lived with us was the exact same age as Maisie's mom, who lived in Kansas. Maisie loved my mom and spent time with her. Once I came home from homeschool co-op to find Maisie and my mom having white wine and chicken sandwiches together under a flowering Bradford Pear tree in Maisie's front yard. Maisie had hung coconuts from the branches so that she and my mom could sing "I've Got a Lovely Bunch of Coconuts" (the Danny Kaye, 1951 version) as a duet. After a few glasses of wine, this song was pretty crazy and could be heard down the block. Maisie knew I was busy with homeschooling, and since her children were in private school and college and her mom many miles away, she decided to invest her time in my mom.

We were honest friends, and that honesty always felt risky and dangerous. We cried over our differences, and we clung to our friendship.

And then Maisie and Mary Jo moved to the West Coast, and Kent and I moved to North Carolina.

When Maisie made a surprise visit, it was like she had never left. We laughed. We cried. And we talked immediately about politics and faith.

Maisie started it. (She always did.)

"I can't believe your stupid governor and that horrible HB2!" (HB2 is the famous bathroom bill in North Carolina that declared people should use only the restroom and locker room that matches the sex listed on their birth certificate.)

"Governor McCrory is such a hater!" Maisie exclaimed.

This wasn't just politics to Maisie.

I remember.

I remember that deep pit of fear that accompanied laws, bills, and policies that failed to uphold LGBTQ rights. Romans 1:32 is never far from my heart these days: "Though they know God's righteous decree, that those who practice such things deserve to die, they not only do them, but give approval to those who practice them." When you are in the LGBTQ community, you measure all friendships and all events by one yardstick: Do you give approval to me? Approval from others feels like life or death. The Bible makes clear that if you cannot receive a blessing from God, you will demand it from human beings. And no person—no bill, no policy, no civil right—is big enough to compensate for God's lack. So you hold the line with violence. Failing to approve LGBTQ legislation feels like a failure to recognize your personhood. This rejection cuts as deep as it can.

A lot had happened since the days that we were neighbors.

Since the LGBTQ community had won the conditional right to gay marriage, religious liberty fallouts were beginning. SOGI (sexual orientation gender identity) laws were popping up everywhere. Building on Obergefell, SOGI laws demand that sexual orientation be recognized as a separate category of personhood. This means that under the law, a person who identifies as lesbian, gay, bisexual, or transgender is seen as a separate kind of person, with distinct rights and privileges and protections. The Bible understands how LGBTQ may describe *how you feel* (and how you perceive life and ideas and events). Our doctrine of sin explains that. But under God's economy, LGBTQ will never describe *who you are*, because feelings that orient you toward sinful actions are not ontological (original to the core of who you are). Who you are is an image bearer of a holy God, called to reflect God in knowledge, righteousness, and holiness, with a soul that will last forever, for glory or for judgment. The Bible does not recognize sexual orientation as a category of personhood. Sexual orientation was Freud's nineteenth-century invention. The Bible understands that after Adam, we have a sin orientation, all of us. And for some of us, that sin orientation comes with same-sex attraction (SSA).

The biblical gospel is on a collision course with the worldview that my friend fought for.

Either sexual orientation is a true reflection of personhood, or it is a Freudian category mistake.

If sexual orientation is a form of personhood, inherent to one's dignity of self and of expression, how could the gospel be good news for people who identify as LGBTQ? Why does the good news of the Bible always come with death to the person you once were (Gal. 2:20)?

The stakes are as high as they can be.

I only asked Maisie one question.

"Maisie, how is your heart?"

"Dreadful. I'm garbage. My wife despises me." Maisie's voice trickled into a whisper of shame. All of the political rallies, all of the fights for policy and progress, it all came down to nothing. Maisie was defeated. She looked lost, gone, unmoored.

I walked over and put my arms around my friend.

"Maisie, Jesus would never treat you like this. Jesus treats his daughters like royalty. Jesus asks a lot, I know, but he gives you the world."

It was hard to say so little. It has been hard to pray so much more than I say.

————

REFLECTIONS ON THIS STORY AND ONGOING STORIES

The friendship of a good neighbor can run deep and wide. But what if your daughter, raised in a Christian home, returns from college radicalized by the LGBTQ community? What if she comes out as pansexual and tells you under no uncertain terms that it is her way or the highway? What if you discover that your most obedient and faithful daughter, the one you never had to worry about with boys or drugs or reckless bad-choice making, has been struggling with same-sex attraction since she was twelve? What if she leaves you—betrays you—for a church that makes peace between her deepest desires and her Christian faith? What if she takes aim at all that you believe on social media? What if, armed with the philosophy of the Gay Christian Network, she accuses you of playing the role of a modern-day Pharisee for upholding the moral law of God? What if she believes that you are in sin for withholding affirmation of same-sex sexual love?

Some believe that we live in the midst of a moral revolution, with "liquid modernism" flooding into the bulwarks and mainstays of post-Christian cultures.[2] Others call this sort of talk "alarmist" and believe that we live in the days of happy progress, where we can finally realize a true melting pot of human potential. No one feels this tension more than Christian parents whose children are, for a season—perhaps for a very long season—lost to the LGBTQ community and its values.

I believe that we are living in the midst of a moral revolution.

Sadly, this is the revolution that I helped launch.

Blogger Tim Challies, quoting from Theo Hobson in *Reinventing Liberal Christianity*, gives us this yardstick to measure the times. A moral and sexual revolution has three benchmarks:

1. What was universally condemned is now celebrated.
2. What was universally celebrated is now condemned.
3. Those who refuse to celebrate are condemned.[3]

I believe that we have met benchmark numbers 1 and 2, and that we are just at the beginning of number 3.

It is deeply frightening when a child you have loved and raised and prayed for daily leaves the faith, and with it, God's protection. It can feel shameful to admit to others in your church that you are torn between your faith and your child—that you fear losing one for the other. It may feel unsafe to ask for help from your elders and pastors with matters that isolate you and set you apart from others in painful ways. You may feel jealous or angry or deeply depressed that while your peers in the church are planning biblical weddings for believing children, you are wrestling with whether to attend the gay wedding of your prodigal. If these are your feelings and concerns, take heart. The Lord is near.

Two helpful resources for you are Christopher Yuan and Angela Yuan, *Out of the Far Country: A Gay Son's Journey to God; A Broken Mother's Search for Hope*,[4] and a workshop by HarvestUSA (harvestusa.org) entitled "Raising Sexually Healthy Children."[5] *Out of a Far Country* is a powerful memoir about the power of prayer and God's love. It is a must-read for parents with children lost for a season to the LGBTQ community. Harvest USA is a sexual brokenness ministry that offers a transformative workshop for churches, along with other resources for people who struggle with SSA. The workshops help elders and pastors identify and change a toxic church culture, and to become a body of Christ that is safe for people to share how they struggle and what they need. These workshops also equip parents of young children to prepare them for the world that we now inhabit.

Or perhaps you feel the weight of others in your church who struggle with same-sex attraction and are faithful members of your church, forsaking sin and living in chastity, but still feeling torn between the culture of the church and the culture of the world. You may feel as if all your Christian friends do is make straw arguments *against* homosexuality—declaring it a choice and a bad choice, and demanding that real believers won't struggle with *that* struggle. You may be sick and tired of hearing "arguments against" something and are hungering for the Jesus who *argues for* people, and who beckons and promises comfort for bruised reeds.

Or perhaps you are someone who also struggles with SSA. You are silent, though, and the hateful things people in your church say make you more silent every day. Your shame may be increasing as you are saying to yourself: *If they only knew how I feel and how I struggle, they would kick me out for good.* You may wonder if you will ever hear these words of Jesus in real time: "Come to me, all who labor and are heavy laden, and I will give you rest. Take my yoke upon you, and learn from me, for I am gentle and lowly in heart, and you will find rest for your souls. For my yoke is easy, and my burden is light" (Matt. 11:28–30). This is a painful reality for so many sisters in the church. If you are someone struggling with SSA in God's way—forsaking sin, drinking deeply of the means of grace—then you are a hero of the faith. Nothing less.

If this is your burden, then the Bible has the answer for it.

The practice of daily, ordinary, radical hospitality.

Where should you start?

As a church community, designate a house where members live and where people can gather daily. Yes, I said daily. And then start gathering daily. And not by invitation only.

Make it a place where the day closes with a meal for all, and with Bible reading and prayer, and where unbelievers are invited to hear the words of grace and salvation, where children of all ages are welcome, and where unbelievers and believers break bread and ideas shoulder to shoulder.

This is the best way that I know of to evangelize your LGBTQ neighbors—and everyone else. To live communally as Bible-believing Christians who care for each other in body and soul. To live openly, such that you know each other well enough to know each other's sin patterns and temptations. To be a community where everyone is repenting of something all the time. To be a community where Christ could come, eat, wash his feet, and lay down his head. To be a community where hard conversations are had over warm soup and fresh bread. You see, two hours on a Sunday morning and two hours at a small group on Tuesday night is not enough. God so loves you that he wants you to live 24/7 as a Christ follower, doing the will of God from the heart and the home.

Maybe this seems pie-in-the-sky crazy. Maybe it is.

But this is the kind of house in which I first saw the gospel lived and loved.

And, by God's grace, this is the kind of house in which I now live.

The best way to evangelize your LGBTQ neighbors is to get upstream of the culture war—and to stay there. And practicing daily, ordinary, radical hospitality is the way to do that.

In a culture of biblical hospitality, we develop real friendships.

We talk about our differences as grown-ups who can understand each other's point of view even if we don't share it. We understand why people who cannot have eternal peace are driven to accumulate rights and privileges to compensate for this. We know that the accumulation of rights and privileges causes great anxiety within the LGBTQ community, especially when you are winning. The potential blow of losing that which you have is far greater than never having something. Without the gospel's checks and balances on the things of this world, you are awash in anxiety in a nanosecond.

When we meet a neighbor who identifies within the spectrum of LGBTQ life and identity, we do not presume that she is sexually active. She may be, but celibacy is high in the lesbian community. So we commit ourselves to listening, and to treating each person we meet as an individual.

We understand that sins of identity run deep and hard.

Coming to faith in Jesus Christ in 1999 caused a cavernous identity crisis. I felt that I had to leave not only a woman I loved but also a worldview I loved. I had believed that my sexuality as a lesbian was cleaner and more moral because it did not include penetration of any kind. When Christians told me I was in sin, I don't think they understood the comprehensive nature of my feelings and life. I was not only same-sex attracted. I was also opposite-sex repelled. The idea of vaginal penetration made me feel kind of queasy. And when I came to Christ, I broke up with my partner because I knew that obedience to Christ was commanded. But my heart was not in it. Not at all. And conversion to Christ did not initially change my sexual attraction to women. What conversion did change was my heart and mind. My mind was on fire for the Bible, and I could not read enough of it or enough about it. And my heart was comforted and encouraged by my time—almost daily—in the home of Ken and Floy Smith. The Smiths took me in. But—I was not converted out of homosexuality. I was converted out of unbelief.

Daily Bible reading and daily Christian community made me

understand something: union with Christ was emerging as a central component to my identity, one that competed with my sexual identity. Ken and Floy Smith discipled me in what it means to bear the image of God. From the minute they met me—as a gay-rights activist—they treated me like an image bearer of a holy God, with a soul that will last forever.

How do we evangelize our LGBTQ neighbors? We remind our neighbors that only the love of Christ is seamless. Not so for our spouses or partners. Only Christ loves us best: he took on all our sin, died in our place bearing God's wrath, and rose victorious from the dead. And yes, Christ calls us to be citizens of a new world, under his lordship, under his protection, under his law. Original sin explains why some struggle with same-sex attraction and have from the day they remember being attracted to anything. We know that we were all born in original sin and that this imprints our deepest desires. As we grow in Christ, we gain victory over acting on our sin, but our sinful desires do not go away until glory. And we stand in the risen Christ alone, in his righteousness, not in our own. But we are called—by the God who loves us enough to die for us and live for us—to carry a cross, repent of sin, and follow him. Christians know that crosses are not curses, not for the believer.

And Christ puts the lonely in families (Ps. 68:6)—and he calls us to live in a new family of choice: God's family.

So we evangelize the LGBTQ family by living differently than others, by living without selfishness or guile. We tell each other the promise found in Mark 10:28–30—the hundredfold promise—and we bear out its truth in our homes:

Peter began to say to Jesus, "See, we have left everything and followed you."

> Jesus said, "Truly, I say to you, there is no one who has left house or brothers or sisters or mother or father or children or lands, for my sake and for the gospel, who will not *receive a hundredfold* now in this time, houses and brothers and sisters

and mothers and children and lands, with persecutions, and in the age to come eternal life."

Receive a hundredfold.

The gospel promises that our neighbors who leave the LGBTQ community for Christ will receive a hundredfold blessing of new family in Christ. From where will this hundredfold come? Will it drop from the sky? No. It comes not only through the presence of Christ in us but also from individual Christian families and from the body of Christ as found in the local church. This means that while there is solitude, there is no chronic loneliness. This means that birthdays and holidays are spent with your family of God. This means that you are known and you know. This means that you live a life filled with godly intimacy. If the church is not ready to deliver on this hundredfold promise, to what are we calling our friends? I know what we are calling them *from*, but *to* what are we calling them?

You see, I believe that the gospel comes with a house key.[6]

I believe that if Christians lived differently, communally, then people who struggle with same-sex attraction would not be driven away from the church for intimacy, but instead would find real intimacy within the family of God. If we really believed that the blood of Christ is thicker than the blood of biology, or that partaking of the Lord's Supper together is the highest bond of intimacy people can have, we would see and deal with each other differently. We would stop regarding singles as people who need to be fixed or fixed up. We would understand that biblical marriage points to the marriage of Christ and the church. We would appreciate that while marriage is by God's design, he did not design every person for biblical marriage. At the same time, all Christians are married to Christ, have union with Christ, and will be fulfilled only in the new Jerusalem.

This is the question that we who wish to evangelize the LGBTQ community must answer: *To what are we calling people?* If we know what we are calling people from, but do not have anything to call people to, we are only sharing half of the gospel. The LGBTQ community is a real community, and too often the church survives on a starvation diet of community. This hypocrisy is not lost on the watching world.

10

Spreading the Word in Diverse Contexts

Women All around You

INTRODUCING THE STORIES—
A NOTE FROM THE EDITORS

This chapter aims to celebrate and encourage the sharing of the gospel by those of one national or cultural background with those of a different one. The beautiful motivation for cross-cultural evangelism is that all the nations belong to Jesus. Psalm 2:8 lets us hear God the Father speaking to God the Son, saying: "Ask of me, and I will make the nations your heritage, and the ends of the earth your possession." Jesus does ask, and his Father gives him the nations. "And people will come from east and west, and from north and south, and recline at table in the kingdom of God" (Luke 13:29).

The rule of Christ over all the nations has been God's plan from before the foundations of the earth. The Old Testament points to this plan with growing clarity—from the promise to Abraham that in him all the families of the earth would be blessed (Gen. 12:3); to the remarkable enfolding into Israel of figures like Rahab (in Joshua 2), Ruth, and Naaman the commander of the army of Aram (in 2 Kings 5); to the many servants and captives who joined the nation of Israel along the way. The prophet Isaiah pictured all the nations going up to the mountain of the Lord God (Isa. 2:1–3).

The seed of Abraham became a nation from whose people came King Jesus—who died to redeem a people called from all the nations of the world. The apostle Peter didn't understand this until God sent him a vision and a message from Cornelius, a Gentile believer who illustrated the truth Peter then proclaimed: "Truly I understand that God shows no partiality, but in every nation anyone who fears him and does what is right is acceptable to him" (Acts 10:34–35; for context, see Acts 10:1–48). Peter went on to explain the means of God's acceptance: faith in the death and resurrection of the promised Lord Jesus Christ. "To him all the prophets bear witness that everyone who believes in him receives forgiveness of sins through his name" (Acts 10:43).

Just this brief review lights up Jesus's parting command to his disciples to go and make disciples of all nations (Matt. 28:19), bearing witness from Jerusalem to the ends of the earth (Acts 1:8). Most readers of this book probably represent the non-Jewish peoples to whom the gospel has indeed spread. And there are still more unreached people groups who have not heard. Jesus told his disciples that "this gospel of the kingdom will be proclaimed throughout the whole world as a testimony to all nations, and then the end will come" (Matt. 24:14). This is a worldwide commission that God's people hold. It's a commission meant to cross cultural and national boundaries. We're heading for a kingdom made up of a multitude "from every nation, from all tribes and peoples and languages, standing before the throne and before the Lamb," all singing praise to him for his great salvation (Rev. 7:9–12).

This book does not address the organized missionary enterprises that have aimed and are aiming today to reach all the nations with the gospel. As God's people, we must take part in these enterprises through support and prayer and sending and going—in the various combinations God puts before us. But before us all, God puts opportunities to reach the nations through bearing witness to the people around us, wherever we are. That bearing witness is what the following stories illustrate. We thank the treasured friends who have contributed these stories, and pray for increased fruit and blessing in their lives. We hope these stories will encourage and inspire more and more bold bearing witness to Christ among the nations by God's people near and far. We hope these stories will encourage us all to pray for more and more stories such as this to tell.[1]

The first story is told by a woman living in the suburbs of a city in the midwestern United States.

SHARING A HOME WITH THE NATIONS

Several years ago, our church was making a concerted effort to focus on adoption. My kids were in high school and college, and the thought of starting over with children seemed daunting. But my heart was stirred. I began to pray, not really knowing what I was praying for. Soon our youngest daughter, who was attending a Christian high school, asked my husband and me to think about hosting an international student in our home for the school year. This was the answer I was looking for. I could care for another girl, but it was only a school-year-long commitment. This was perfect. My husband was totally on board as were the rest of our children. We went through the training and inspection, and we were all set to host one student. Then the program director asked us to take on two girls—and by mid-year, three!

Two of our girls were from China and one from Vietnam. Only one was a Christian. We loved the missional aspect of this program. Not only were these girls going to classes; they were in Bible classes and rubbing shoulders daily with Christian students. Our atheist Chinese "daughter," Lily, was hearing about God and Christianity for the first time in her life. Often we would be in the kitchen preparing dinner together, and she would ask, "Now what are the steps you have to take to become a Christian?" or "So God, Jesus, and the Holy Spirit are the same thing?" It was so refreshing for all of us and so exciting to be explaining our faith. It pushed us away from the esoteric and toward the basic and beautiful truths of our faith. The whole family was involved.

I told Lily that putting her faith in Christ was a life-changing decision, and she should not go into it lightly. She would know when/if it would be time to become a Christian. A few months later, her school brought in a Christian professor from the Harvard Business School to speak to all the students. He later spoke to the international students about Christianity, addressing the specific questions she had regarding being a Christian in China. When he asked if anyone wanted to become a Christian, Lily's hand was the first one up. Several other students followed Jesus that day. My own high school daughter was at school to bring Lily home. She was the first person Lily told of her decision. I think my daughter *flew* home, so excited was she for us to hear the news. It was wonderful and genuine. As the school year came to an end, we talked with Lily about ways to explain this to her family and how she might handle different situations over the summer break.

Lily was able to explain her new commitments to her mother during a visit her mother made to the United States in order to help Lily evaluate various colleges and universities. We're delighted that Lily is attending a college nearby, and last year she got plugged in to a small, Bible-believing church that she chose on her own. She invited us to her baptism, where we got to see her proclaim her faith to all her friends and her American family.

We went into hosting international students with baby steps. We didn't know what we were doing, but we wanted to treat these girls as we would want our own girls treated if they went to a different country. We wanted to get to know them well and meet their needs, and we thought this would be a one-year commitment. We are now in year five, and we love it. Out of the seven different girls we have hosted, we have seen three become believers (three were already believers). Living out our faith day in and day out with teenage girls whom we never knew until they joined our family is humbling and rewarding. What started as a stirring from God has not only changed three girls' lives eternally (and potentially the lives of their family members); it has also changed our own family's story, and each of our lives. We've seen the gospel at work at home.

The second story comes from an American housewife living in Asia.

WEEPING WITH THOSE WHO WEEP

Jen was surprised (yet not surprised) by her friend Samirah's response to her tears. Both women are expatriates, brought by work to live in a country other than their native ones. When a massive fire swept through an iconic building in Samirah's hometown, the story was all over the regional news. Jen thought about how sad and demoralized she might feel if the most recognizable, beloved building in her country were suddenly reduced to ashes. Images from the news showed ash-covered pedestrians stumbling through the street; many firefighters had lost their lives. Moved to tears and prayer, Jen texted Samirah that afternoon, "I saw the tower on the news. So heartbreaking."

The following day, Jen walked her son to his kindergarten class and ran into Samirah. Tears sprang into Jen's eyes again as she listened to Samirah describe how she had spent the evening calling her friends and family at home. Everyone was so upset by what had happened.

Then Samirah interrupted herself, "I cried all night. But I don't understand why you would weep for my people?"

Jen knew that the political tension between her home country and Samirah's often produced callousness among the people. She explained to Samirah that it didn't matter to her who it was that experienced loss because her heart was changed by Jesus, she was often moved to tears over the brokenness people experience—even strangers.

"Jesus wept for his friends and his enemies," Jen said.

"I just can't believe that" was Samirah's response.

Jen and Samirah had discussed on a separate occasion how Jen's religious beliefs did not allow for her to hate people from particular countries. This too stunned Samirah.

In the simple (yet profound) command for believers in the resurrected Jesus to "weep with those who weep," Jen saw the precise intersection between her faith in Christ and the darkness of a world that grieves without hope. As her friendship with Samirah continues, Jen is praying that her friend will see and hear more and more evidence to believe that Jesus Christ is the Messiah who changes people from the inside out.

———

The third story (or cluster of stories) comes from an American woman who teaches and helps with childcare in an ESL (English as a second language) program hosted at her church in an American city.

LEARNING LANGUAGE AND MORE

Alaleh is from Iran. She came to the United States twenty years ago, with some background in English, so it wasn't long before she graduated out of ESL classes. But Alaleh came back to volunteer in the early-childhood program, caring for the children of others studying English. We worked together for a full year with four- and five-year-olds in the morning and toddlers in the afternoon. She learned the Christian songs that I taught the children and heard the Bible stories. In the afternoons while the children usually napped, we had time to talk together about many things—and we soon became friends.

One day Alaleh asked if she could ask me a question.

I said, "Of course, anything!"

She said, "How does your faith affect your daily life?"

Wow! I had been praying for an opportunity to share more directly about Christ as Savior. My first response to her was an honest one: that sometimes it didn't affect my day-to-day life as completely as it should, but that the more I understood God's grace, the more I wanted to do God's will in every part of my life. We began to look at Scripture together day after day, as soon as the babies were sleeping, seeing the righteousness of Christ as the way to acceptance with God. Alaleh began to understand Jesus as her hope, Jesus as her rest, Jesus as her peace. We continued to search Scripture together, and it was two years later when my friend put her faith in Jesus as her Savior. God continues to work in her life, as Alaleh shares the gospel with her Muslim family members and as God continues to grow her faith in the one who died for her!

For a few years I provided ESL transportation to a Bantu Somali woman named Uba. After years of persecution and slavery, Uba made her way to a refugee camp in Kenya. She arrived there in 1994 and received refugee status in 2001, but that status was delayed after the 9/11 attacks. She and her family arrived in the United States late in 2002 and learned how to navigate life here: Uba learned slowly but watched her children make great progress. After a few years of attending the ESL classes, her oldest son started attending community college, so I offered to drive Uba, her four-year-old daughter, and her three grandchildren to ESL classes to enable them to continue studying. We talked about her life and mine as we traveled together. We shared stories about our daughters' upcoming weddings—which provided great opportunities for me to talk about what God's Word teaches about marriage.

Eventually we walked together into my church with her four little ones. Uba found in my church a place where she was invited in with a warm welcome, where she felt safe, and where she was treated with love. At Christmas she heard the story of the incarnation. She regularly heard the gospel as she came back again and again. The following year, I helped connect her with Re:new, a sewing ministry, where she continued to hear about Jesus through her relationships with other believers there. Uba doesn't know Jesus as her Lord yet, but she knows many things about him and his gift of salvation. And she knows me and knows I love her and her family—and that I pray for her.

One of my favorite stories involves a shy, four-year-old Nepali girl named Priyatama, who in five months in our ESL program had only spoken a few words. Her mom was so happy to have her in school. One day I crossed paths with the little girl and her parents at a grocery store. I hadn't ever met her dad before. Priyatama was so puzzled to see me out of context. (I think in a child's mind, teachers live in their classrooms!) As the mom explained who I was to her husband (in Nepali), Priyatama started singing our prayer from snack time: "God our Father, God our Father, we thank you, we thank you, for our many blessings, for our many blessings. Amen, amen." The mom then explained to me, in very simple English, that Priyatama has her family sing that song at meals at home. We had never heard her sing a word of it at school, and yet she had learned it almost perfectly! It encouraged all of us who share truths from God's Word with the children, that God is faithful and his Word does not return void!

––––––––––

The fourth story comes from a woman who with her husband min-
isters to people of the Muslim faith in a large US city. They live
near their Muslim friends, and they share not only faith but life
with them.

TURKISH COFFEE NIGHTS AND TALKING ABOUT JESUS

Being willing to go to our Muslim friends' homes, community cen-
ters, mosques, and celebrations is key to loving them. Ramadan is
a wonderful time to enter into conversations with Muslims around
us. Often mosque communities in North America will invite non-
Muslims to *Iftar* dinners (breaking-of-the-fast dinners after sunset).
Muslims will sometimes invite their non-Muslim friends over to
experience this important part of their year. These meals feature
traditional foods and long, relaxed conversations.

When we engage with their cultures, we honor Muslims by
learning about what they value. Often within these settings, the
Lord opens opportunities to speak truth about him.

One weekend at a festive "Turkish Coffee Night" amidst cups
of tea, Middle Eastern music, swirling skirts, and tasty pastries,
God provided an encouraging conversation with two of my Muslim
friends, M and O. I'll call myself B.

M: I saw a film in class once about American funerals. There
was drinking and dancing. They said they were celebrating the person's life. Is this normal?

B: A funeral with drinking and dancing? I've never been to one
like that. For Christians, a funeral is a mixture of sadness and hap-
piness. If the person who died was a Christian, we know that they
are in heaven and are now healthy and joyful in God's presence. We
are so happy that they are not sick as they were on earth or struggling with sin. But we are sad for ourselves because we miss their
presence in our lives. I remember when my father's mother died.
She was a Christian. Do you know a song played at Christmas from
Handel's *Messiah*, the "Hallelujah Chorus"? (I sang part of it for

them; they nodded and smiled.) Well, this is not usually at funerals because it's so joyful, but my grandma planned her funeral before she died and she wanted this played at the end. She wanted us to remember she was celebrating in heaven with Jesus!

M and O asked questions about other American funeral traditions, and then they explained the Muslim way.

O: In Islam, all people are buried the same way.

M: Whether rich or poor, man or woman, everyone is wrapped in a white—how do you call it?—cloth, yes. A white cloth, around and around.

O: Their body is put into the ground, and a board is placed over them. Then dirt is put on top. Every Muslim goes to God the same way—no rings, no necklaces, just in the white cloth.

B: May I ask you a question? Do you know if you are going to heaven for sure?

M and O *(in unison and emphatically)*: No! We can't know.

O: Not even our prophet knew if he was going to heaven.

M *(contradicting)*: Yes, he is in heaven.

O: But when the prophet's daughter asked him if he could help her get into heaven, the prophet said he couldn't. . . . We live with a balance of hope and fear. We hope we will get into heaven, but we fear we will go to hell. We hope our good works will be enough on judgment day.

B *(reaching out and touching their arms)*: You know I love you. I think this is the big difference between Christianity and Islam. I know I am going to heaven. I know because of Jesus's work for me. You see, on judgment day, Jesus has offered to stand before God on my behalf. He was perfect. Jesus had no sin. He will stand before God and give me his perfect record. If I stand before God on judgment day with my own record, I will go to hell. I have sin. I struggle with sin every day. But Jesus has offered to give me his perfect record, and so I know I will go to heaven. Does that make sense?

M nodded, understanding registering in her eyes; O turned to another conversation.

M: My friend, I have a question. Is this true for all Christians? Do all Christians go to heaven? I mean, you are close to God. You read the Bible; you teach your children morals; you try to obey God. But what about the Christians who go out at night? What about the Christian women who go from man to man to man?

B: The Bible says that anyone who places their faith in Jesus will go to heaven. But the Bible also says that if we have placed our faith in Jesus, our lives will show it. Because we love Jesus and are thankful to him, we will have works in our lives to show it. These good things do not save us, but they are a result of being saved. When I talk to my children about salvation, I tell them that we ask Jesus to be our Savior and our King. What do we say to a king? If a king asks us to do something, we say yes. We obey.

M: We have something like this in Islam too. We have a saying "Your life shows what you believe."

B: There is something more. If I tried to obey God in my own power, I wouldn't be able to do it. But when we place our faith in Jesus, he sends us God's Holy Spirit. The Holy Spirit gives us the power to obey God. You know, Satan is always tempting us. (M *nodded emphatically.*) Satan is always trying to get us to take the wrong path. But God's Holy Spirit gives us the power to say no to temptation, the power to be protected from Satan. When God's Holy Spirit is inside of us, then we can obey.

Our conversation continued into the evening, talking about the Holy Spirit's empowerment for the challenges of parenting. Eventually it turned to other topics, but I was grateful for the few minutes the Lord had opened to discuss issues of eternal significance. I am thankful for the opportunity to know these friends, and I pray for ongoing opportunities to share Jesus with them.

———

The fifth story comes from an American teacher living in Southeast Asia.

GOD HEARS OUR PRAYERS ABOUT EVANGELISM

As a teacher in a Christian context, I have many opportunities to share the gospel with various students from different countries. But recently I have prayed for God to lead me to more personal conversations and relationships with individuals who don't know Christ—especially the people of the land where I live. In my experience, God answers such prayers pretty quickly. I'll give just one small example.

I prayed specifically one morning for God to direct the various encounters of a rather scattered and busy day and to use me for his gospel purposes. In the late afternoon, I stopped by a busy coffee shop, purchased a green-tea-flavored icy drink, and was just sitting down for a moment to cool off and do a little reading. But just as the iPad came out, along came a relatively new friend of mine, an English-speaking woman from our international church congregation. She was flushed. She apologized profusely for interrupting, but she explained with a rush of words: "I've just had lunch with a friend from this area who's not a Christian, and she's asking me all sorts of hard questions about what I believe and what the Bible says—and I wonder if you could come and help me talk with her!"

It was as if God was smiling and saying, "Well, you asked. Here you go." As it turned out, the conversation my friend and I had with this thoughtful and curious woman was not a smooth one. It was full of hard questions, some of which I'm sure I answered better (and worse!) than others. The woman had heard enough about Christianity to make arguments against it—but I soon discovered what she had not done was to examine the Bible for herself.

"What kind of a God," she asked, "would ask a man to sacrifice his own son like God asked Abraham to do?"

"Do you know the end of that story?" I asked her.

She didn't—and I got to tell her about how God himself provided a lamb for that sacrifice, and about how God has provided the perfect Lamb to pay for our sins in the sacrifice of his own Son.

Toward the end of our long, friendly, intense conversation, this questioner finally said, "Well, I'm happy to believe in Jesus along with all the other gods people tell me about."

In this country, people know stories about a lot of different gods. I encouraged her to sit down and read through the Gospel of John, looking for places where Jesus tells us who he is and what it means to believe in him—and asking whether it would actually be possible to believe in Jesus along with other gods. She was thoughtful. I've prayed she'll sit down and read. I've been in conversation with her friend about other good books to recommend to her as well. We'll talk again perhaps.

I think God used that encounter to teach mainly me. It taught me of his open ear to our prayers. It taught me again of my insufficiency to answer enough questions to bring someone to Christ; only God by his Spirit can open a person's heart and mind to the truth of the gospel. We simply bear witness and pray. We may be one of many who plant seeds. We must not just be ready to give an answer; we must also pray for opportunities to do so. And God will provide them.

———

The sixth story comes from a country in the Middle East.

BRIDGES THROUGH THE WORD

Kiara, a Christian, had several earthly reasons to be intimidated by her coworker, Afareen. Though they are both living abroad and work in the same technology job, their countries of origin are not exactly friendly with one another. Citizens from Kiara's country are looked down upon by those from Afareen's country. Passport-related tension can be so difficult to overcome. Also, Afareen's family problems and explosive bitterness about life made her less approachable than other coworkers. Still, Kiara prayed for Afareen, that God would comfort her in her affliction, meet her in her loneliness, and resolve the many issues that complicate her life.

Kiara read her Bible in the break room at work on many occasions without interruption, but one day Afareen sat at her table and asked, "What are you reading?"

Kiara answered simply, "I'm reading my Bible."

"Why would you want to do that?" Afareen spat back. "God doesn't care. He's probably not even real."

Kiara raised her eyebrow and a question: "Well, have you read the Bible?"

This interaction began weeks of questions and answers that left Kiara rather overwhelmed! Little did Kiara know that Afareen had been searching religious texts online, researching on Google about who Jesus really is—searching for a glimmer of light to relieve the darkness and despair that she felt.

Eventually Afareen started attending church with Kiara and did a Bible study with her in the Gospels, cross-referencing the prophetic literature that the Gospel writers often quote. Afareen became convinced that Jesus is the Messiah and began to follow him. Her family problems have not been resolved yet, but now she is adopted into a new family with a faithful Father and older Brother. And she has gained many, many siblings!

It shall come to pass in the latter days
    that the mountain of the house of the Lord
shall be established as the highest of the mountains,
    and shall be lifted up above the hills;

and all the nations shall flow to it,
      and many peoples shall come and say:
"Come, let us go up to the mountain of the Lord,
      to the house of the God of Jacob,
that he may teach us his ways
      and that we may walk in his paths." (Isa. 2:2–3)

Appendix

Representative Resources
for Evangelism

And I, when I am lifted up from the earth, will draw all people
to myself.

John 12:32

Note from the Editors: This appendix contains a brief list of resources that we have found helpful for encouragement and practical
equipping in spreading the Word. The books and resources here are
by no means an exhaustive list but are representative of the various gifts given by the Spirit for the building up of the church. As
discussed throughout this book, the living and active Word of God
is incomparable. Simply open the Scriptures with your lost friends
and neighbors and read with them. We are also reminded of our
Lord's words concerning the great gift of the Spirit: "Nevertheless,
I tell you the truth: it is to your advantage that I go away, for if I do
not go away, the Helper will not come to you. But if I go, I will send
him to you" (John 16:7). We pray that God's Spirit would guide

and help you as you seek to spread the word of his glorious gospel to the ends of the earth.

————

BeckyPippert.com. *Spreading the Word* contributor Becky Pippert serves internationally in training others for the work of evangelism. Her resources are available via her website and other distributors.

Carson, D. A. *The God Who Is There: Finding Your Place in God's Story*. Grand Rapids, MI: Baker, 2010.

Chapman, John. *A Fresh Start*. New South Wales, Australia: Matthias Media, 2003.

Christianity Explored by CEMinistries. www.ceministries.org/Groups /274683/home/courses/christianity_explored/christianity_explored .aspx. A seven-session study on the Christian faith with various supporting resources available.

Dever, Mark. *The Gospel and Personal Evangelism*. Wheaton, IL: Crossway, 2007.

Gilbert, Greg. *What Is the Gospel?* 9Marks edition. Wheaton, IL: Crossway, 2010.

————. *Who Is Jesus?* Wheaton, IL: Crossway, 2015.

Green, Michael. *Evangelism and the Early Church*. Revised edition. Grand Rapids, MI: Eerdmans, 2004.

Evangelism Bundle by Matthias Media. http://www.matthiasmedia .com/outreach/evangelistic-resources/evangelism-bundle.

Helm, David. *One-to-One Bible Reading*. New South Wales, Australia: Matthias Media, 2010.

Keller, Timothy. *The Reason for God: Belief in an Age of Skepticism*. London: Penguin, 2009.

Packer, J. I. *Evangelism and the Sovereignty of God*. Americanized edition. Downers Grove, IL: InterVarsity Press, 2006.

Piper, John. *50 Reasons Why Jesus Came to Die*. Wheaton, IL: Crossway, 2006.

Pippert, Rebecca Manley. *Out of the Salt Shaker and into the World: Evangelism as a Way of Life*. Revised and expanded edition. Downers Grove, IL: InterVarsity Press, 1999.

Raymond, Erik. Gospel-Shaped Outreach. https://www.thegospel coalition.org/publications/gospel-shaped-outreach. This is a kit of resources for churches on evangelism, from The Gospel Coalition.

Stiles, J. Mack. *Evangelism: How the Whole Church Speaks of Jesus*. Wheaton, IL: Crossway, 2014.

Table Talk games by The Ugly Duckling (Australia). http://www.table -talk.org. These informal games are designed to help facilitate conversations with friends and neighbors.

Two Ways to Live by Matthias Media. http://www.matthiasmedia.com .au/2wtl/whatis2wtl.html. "2WTL" is a gospel presentation that is available via various forms of media.

"What Is the Gospel?" http://www.9marks.org/answer/what-gospel/. This four-point presentation of the gospel is adapted from Mark Dever's book, *The Gospel and Personal Evangelism*.

Who Will Be King? by Matthis Media. http://www.matthiasmedia.com /outreach/two-ways-to-live-resources/who-will-be-king. This is the "Two Ways to Live" gospel presentation for kids.

Contributors

Rosaria Champagne Butterfield was a tenured professor of English and women's studies at Syracuse University when God saved her in 1999 in what she describes as a "train-wreck conversion." Her memoir, *The Secret Thoughts of an Unlikely Convert*, chronicles that difficult journey. Rosaria is married to Kent, a Reformed Presbyterian pastor in North Carolina, and is a homeschool mother, author, and speaker. She is zealous for hospitality, loves her family, cherishes dogs, and enjoys coffee.

Gloria Furman has a MA in Christian Evangelism from Dallas Seminary and lives in Dubai, United Arab Emirates, where her husband serves as the pastor of Redeemer Church of Dubai. They have four children. She is the author of several books, including *Treasuring Christ When Your Hands Are Full*, *Missional Motherhood*, and *Alive in Him*.

Camille Hallstrom has an MFA in Acting from the University of Pittsburgh and an MA in Theology from Covenant Theological Seminary; she is chair of the Theatre Department at Covenant College, Lookout Mountain, Georgia. Most summers find her working for the Church of Uganda and the Episcopal Church of South Sudan in clergy training, prison ministry, and radio broadcast. Occasionally she's been known to find time to perform her one-woman play about Katie von Bora Luther, *Watchmen for the Morning*.

Megan Hill is a pastor's wife and pastor's daughter living in Massachusetts. She is the author of *Praying Together* and is a regular contributor to *Christianity Today*, the Gospel Coalition, and the Christward Collective.

Happy Khambule has been working for thirteen years in one of the hospitals in UAE as a perfusionist. She serves as a deaconess of women's ministry at Redeemer Church of Dubai and enjoys encouraging women to dig deeper into the Word of God. She is married with two sons and two granddaughters.

Jamie Love has been married to Pastor Louis Love Jr. for thirty-nine years, and they have three adult children, two daughters-in-law, and eleven grandchildren. She serves as the director of women's ministries at New Life Fellowship Church in Lake County, Illinois. Jamie is a homeschooler, a speaker, and the cofounder and instructor of a weekly teleconference Bible study and outreach to women across the United States.

Kathleen Nielson (PhD, Vanderbilt University) is an author and speaker who loves working with women in studying the Scriptures. After directing The Gospel Coalition's women's initiatives 2010–2017, she now serves as senior advisor and book editor for TGC. She and her husband, Niel, make their home partly in Wheaton, Illinois, and partly in Jakarta, Indonesia, where Niel leads a network of Christian schools and universities. They have three sons, two daughters-in-law, and five granddaughters.

Becky Pippert is an author, speaker, and founder of Becky Pippert Ministries. She has written numerous books, including *Out of the Salt Shaker*, and holds a BA and MA in English Literature from the University of Illinois. She has done advanced study at the University of Barcelona, Harvard University, and the (former) American Institute in Israel. Becky and her husband, Dick, have ministered on six continents. They have four children and live in Holland, Michigan.

Eowyn Stoddard was raised as a missionary kid in France, studied German at Wellesley College, then received a master's in Theology from Westminster Seminary (CA) where she met her husband, David. They married in 1997 and moved in 2001 as church-planting missionaries to East Berlin—where she currently enjoys the open doors of ministry to refugees. Eowyn and David have five children.

SharDavia Walker lives in Lynchburg, Virginia, and serves on staff with a college ministry, Campus Outreach, as the Regional Women's Director. She and her husband are members at Rivermont Evangelical Presbyterian Church.

Notes

Introduction

1. Beth Urton, Danielle Sallade, Mi Xue, and Kori Porter, "Evangelism: Sharing the Reason for Our Hope" (panel presentation, Together for the Gospel Women's Conference, June 17, 2016), http://resources.thegospelcoalition.org/library/-1fd7c113-1102-4feb-8e85-0f9654f92c20.

Chapter 1: The Glorious *What of Evangelism*

1. The New Age movement (at its height in the 1970s but still manifesting its influence) emphasizes a relatively undefined divinity that is everywhere, including within human beings.
2. John R. W. Stott, *The Cross of Christ* (Downers Grove, IL: InterVarsity, 1986), 160.
3. For his detailed unfolding of these ideas, see Peter Lewis, *The Glory of Christ* (Carlisle, Cumbria, UK: Paternoster, 1992).
4. C. S. Lewis, *The Great Divorce* (New York: Macmillan, 1946), 72–73.

Chapter 2: The Heart of the Evangelist

1. Robert Murray M'Cheyne, quoted in Horatius Bonar, *Words to Winners of Souls* (Pensacola, FL: Chapel Library, n.d.), 8.
2. In this chapter, I use "neighbor" in its broad, biblical sense. Neighbors are friends, relatives, coworkers, moms at the playground, members of unreached people groups, and the family who lives next door. When the lawyer asked Jesus, "Who is my neighbor?" Jesus's answer was clear: Everybody is your neighbor (Luke 10:25–37).
3. J. Todd Billings, *Union with Christ: Reframing Theology and Ministry for the Church* (Grand Rapids, MI: Baker Academic, 2011), 25, emphasis in original.
4. On this point, I highly recommend and am indebted to Jeremy Walker, *The Brokenhearted Evangelist* (Grand Rapids, MI: Reformation Heritage, 2012).
5. J. C. Ryle, *Practical Religion* (Grand Rapids, MI: Baker, 1977), 133–34.
6. Albert Mohler, "The Power of the Articulated Gospel" (main session lecture, Together for the Gospel conference, April 11, 2012), http://t4g.org/media/2012/05/the-power-of-the-articulated-gospel-2/.

7. Matthew Henry, *Matthew Henry's Commentary: Job to Song of Solomon,* vol. 3 (1710; repr., Peabody, MA: Hendrickson, 1991), 807.

8. Dick McLellan, *Warriors of Ethiopia: Heroes of the Gospel in the Omo River Valley* (Kingsway, Australia: Kingsgrove, 2006), 171.

9. The Westminster Shorter Catechism defines prayer as "an offering up of our desires unto God, for things agreeable to his will." *Westminster Shorter Catechism,* quoted in *The Confessions of Faith Together with the Larger Catechism and the Shorter Catechism with Scripture Proofs,* 3rd ed. (Lawrenceville, GA: Christian Education & Publications, 1990), Q&A 98.

10. Bonar, *Words to Winners,* 9.

11. Robert Murray M'Cheyne, quoted in Andrew Bonar, *Robert Murray M'Cheyne* (repr., 2012; Edinburgh: Banner of Truth, 1844), 160.

12. Mohler, "The Power."

13. C. H. Spurgeon, *The Soul Winner* (repr., Pasadena, TX: Pilgrim Publications, 2007), 45.

14. Hughes Oliphant Old, "Assembly Required," in *The Communion of Saints: Living in Fellowship with the People of God,* ed. Philip Graham Ryken (Phillipsburg, NJ: P&R, 2001), 74.

15. Bonar, *Words to Winners,* 16.

Chapter 3: The Cultural Mandate and the Great Commission

1. More from the letter: "My fear for [the students], of course, is that since the *faculty* offered them this activity, they will (in a typical twenty-something, braggadocio fashion) unthinkingly assume "they can handle it." Of course, they don't even know what "it" is, much less that "it" is something no human being was ever designed to handle. Pray that the faculty will have wisdom to see that if we are thoughtless in our approach to training students, we might actually *cauterize*, not *develop* their immature artistic/spiritual apparatus. Pray [for the man who directed this play]. . . . I think he suspects that one of the student-actresses was harmed by the work. God give him eyes to see. (The particular actress in question is a Christian. I called her into my office after I saw the show and asked her about her experience. She'd found it quite traumatic. Still, apparently, the director *had* asked her more than once if she was 'ok' with doing the show, and unfortunately she did not have the gumption to tell him 'no.' To me, she said that she'd feared she couldn't get through the run of the show. . . .). Pray that God will give this and other students wisdom to stand on their principles, for the glory of God. I think this student was wrong not to have told the director the truth. Unfortunately, I also think she was *wronged* to have ever been put in the position where she'd have to make such a choice. 'Bucking the system' may be a choice Christian students have to make at times, but having wisdom to know when to do it is hard. Students are between a rock and a hard place—they must *obey* the educational authorities if they wish to learn, but they also need to know when to say 'no' if a teacher hands them an inappropriate assignment. It is not just for students to find themselves in such situations. . . . It is impossible that they will have suf-

ficient wisdom to make right choices unless God grants it to them." (Camille J. Hallstrom, "Theatre as Incarnation: Toward a Vision for Redemption of Dramatic Art," *Presbyterion: Covenant Seminary Review* 27, no. 2: 144, http://studyres.com/doc/7954515/theatre-as-incarnation-toward-a-vision-for.

2. H. R. Rookmaaker, *Modern Art and the Death of a Culture* (Wheaton, IL: Crossway, 1994), 136.

3. Francis A. Schaeffer, *The God Who Is There* (Downers Grove, IL: InterVarsity Press, 1968), 129, 142.

4. Hilary Brand and Adrienne Chaplin, *Art and Soul, Signposts for Christians in the Arts*, 2nd ed. (Downers Grove, IL: InterVarsity, 2001), 7, 15.

5. Cf. "Even if some do not obey the word, they may be won without a word . . . when they see your respectful and pure conduct. . . . [But always be] prepared to make a defense to anyone who asks you for a reason for the hope that is in you" (1 Pet. 3:1–2, 15).

6. Material for these two paragraphs is adapted from Hallstrom, "Theatre as Incarnation," 146.

7. Wording is taken from Dramatist Play Service's license for nonprofessional performance rights.

8. Margaret Edson, *Wit* (New York: Dramatists Play Service, 1999), 14.

9. Edson, *Wit*, 14.

10. Deference to the privacy of actors and audience was maintained in staging. Vivian lay on the exam table, her head angled slightly toward the audience, her stirruped feet slightly away. Medical drapery provided sufficient "willing suspension of disbelief" that a pelvic exam could be "seen" by the audience without actually being realistically enacted.

11. Mart Green and Steve Saint, "The End of the Spear Controversy: Mart Green and Steve Saint Offer Answers," Eternal Perspective Ministries website, February 21, 2006, http://www.epm.org/resources/2006/Feb/21/end-spear -controversy-mart-green-and-steve-saint-o.

12. Randy Alcorn, "Perspectives on End of the Spear and the Chad Allen Controversy," Eternal Perspective Ministries website, February 1, 2006, http:// www.epm.org/resources/2006/Feb/01/perspectives-end-spear-and-chad-allen -controversy. After speaking wisely into the controversy, Alcorn added: "And pray for Chad Allen that he would be brought to the end of himself (as all of us need to be, regardless of which sins we happen to embrace and advocate). And that Chad may be drawn into a real relationship with Jesus Christ. How I would love to one day embrace him as my brother."

13. "Excerpt from an Interview with Chad Allen," *The DQ Times*, accessed April 14, 2012, http://thedqtimes.com/pages/castpages/other/chadendofthespear interview.htm.

Chapter 4: Mercy Ministry and Proclamation Ministry

1. "Proclamation and mercy" will be used interchangeably with "word and deed," "truth and mercy," and "speaking and serving."

2. "Mission is, by definition, 'holistic,' and therefore 'holistic mission' is,

de facto, mission. Proclamation alone, apart from any social concern, may be perceived as a distortion, a truncated version of the true gospel, a parody and travesty of the good news, lacking relevance for the real problems of real people living in the real world. On the other end of the spectrum, exclusive focus on transformation and advocacy may just result in social and humanitarian activism, void of any spiritual dimension. Both approaches are unbiblical; they deny the wholeness of human nature of human beings created in the image of God. Since we are created whole, and since the fall affects our total humanity in all its dimensions, then redemption, restoration, and mission can, by definition, only be 'holistic.'" Jean Paul Heldt, "Revisiting the Whole Gospel: Toward a Biblical Model of Holistic Mission in the 21st Century," *Missiology* 32 (2004): 166.

3. *Physical Needs*: God, in his goodness, created a world in which the basic human needs for oxygen, water, food, shelter, and sleep can be met. These are gifts all humans enjoy. We have the capacity to care for the needs of others in self-sacrificing ways because we are made in God's likeness.

   Relational Needs: Our relational needs are important for human thriving and surviving. Studies have shown that infants who receive food without love expressed in human touch or speech fail to thrive, and in some cases even die. We imitate the triune God when we live in relationship expressing love, care, and life-giving words to one another.

   Spiritual Needs: The Bible places a heavy emphasis on a singular, *ultimate* need. God placed eternity in every human heart. This means that no material thing, no human relationship, could ever fill the black hole of need in our hearts that which God intended to fill himself.

4. Jesus understood this. Taxes were due to Caesar because his image was on the denarius (Matt. 22:15–22).

5. Health is not a guarantee for a Christian. Sometimes God heals, and sometimes he has plans to use sickness in our life to teach us how to lean on him. But perfect health is coming one day!

6. "For your Maker is your husband—the Lord Almighty is his name—the Holy One of Israel is your Redeemer; he is called the God of all the earth" (Isa. 54:5 NIV) and "'Return, faithless people,' declares the Lord, 'for I am your husband'" (Jer. 3:14 NIV).

7. The tokens Jesus gave us to remember his work are the sacraments of baptism and the Lord's Supper.

8. Hebrew term for helpmeet, suitable helper, or necessary ally.

9. W. L. Westermann, "Notes upon the Ephodia of Greek Ambassadors," *Classical Philology*, 5, no. 2 (1910): 203–16.

10. The other three main passages describing the spiritual gifts are Romans 12:6–8; 1 Corinthians 12:4–11; and 1 Corinthians 12:28.

11. Speaking or proclamation gifts are teaching, preaching, prophecy, discernment, knowledge, speaking in tongues, interpreting tongues, evangelism, encouragement, intercession, and by extrapolation, Peter's own writing of letters.

12. Gifts of service or mercy are material and financial giving, hospitality, healing,

administration, executing justice, and practical help of all sorts. "In all things I have shown you that by working hard in this way we must help the weak and remember the words of the Lord Jesus, how he himself said, 'It is more blessed to give than to receive'" (Acts 20:35).

13. The early church in Acts continues the work of Jesus both in proclaiming the Word and deeds of mercy. One of the first reactions of new converts that we see in Acts is bringing belongings and earned income from the sales of fields before the apostles' feet. Caring for those in need among the new family of faith became a big issue that led to the appointment of deacons who could oversee the fair distribution of help to widows and others in need.

14. Christopher Wright, *The Mission of God: Unlocking the Bible's Grand Narrative* (Downers Grove, IL: InterVarsity Press, 2006), 319.

15. Thomas Manton, *The Complete Works of Thomas Manton, D.D.*, vol. 17 (London: J. Nisbet & Company, 1974), 150.

16. For the full story, see Nik Ripken, "What's Wrong with Western Missionaries?" Desiring God website, September 12, 2016, http://www.desiringgod.org /articles/what-s-wrong-with-western-missionaries.

Chapter 5: Spreading the Word in Everyday Life

1. C. S. Lewis, *The Weight of Glory* (San Francisco, CA: HarperOne, 2001), 45–46.

2. Please see the appendix for a list of helpful resources such as the ones I've mentioned.

3. Augustine, *Confessions*, I, 1.

4. Maltbie D. Babcock, "This Is My Father's World" (1901).

Chapter 6: Spreading the Word among Children

1. Colin Smith, "The Conveniently Neglected Teachings of Jesus—Family Part 2" (audio message, *Unlocking the Bible* broadcast, June 1, 2012), http://unlocking thebible.org/broadcast/family-part-2/.

2. Samuel Ward Hutton, *Minister's Service Manual: Updated and Expanded* (Grand Rapids, MI: Baker, 2003), 164–65.

3. James Cameron, "Biblically Training Children, I," in *A Theology of the Family*, ed. Jeff Pollard and Scott Brown (Wake Forest, NC: National Center for Family-Integrated Churches), 414.

4. Eugene H. Peterson, *A Long Obedience in the Same Direction* (Downers Grove, IL: InterVarsity Press, 2000).

5. Clara Teare Williams, "Satisfied" (1875).

6. This section is adapted from Louis Love, "Summer Means Good Times" The Front Porch website, August 19, 2015, http://thefrontporch.org/2015/08 /summer-means-good-times/. This adaptation is included with the permission of Louis C. Love Jr.

7. Quoted in *A Theology of the Family*, ed. Jeff Pollard and Scott Brown (Wake Forest, NC: National Center for Family-Integrated Churches), 340.

Chapter 7: Spreading the Word among University Students

1. The terms "college" and "university" do have technically different meanings; however, in conversation these terms are often used interchangeably—as I will do.
2. All names have been changed for the sake of privacy.

Chapter 8: Spreading the Word in the Workplace

1. This email has been minimally edited for punctuation, etc.

Chapter 9: Spreading the Word among Friends Identifying as LGBTQ

1. Most names, places, and settings have been changed for people's privacy and protection.
2. An excellent articulation of this can be found in Rod Dreher's *The Benedict Option: A Strategy for Christians in a Post-Christian Nation* (New York: Sentinel [Penguin Random House], 2017).
3. Tim Challies, "Final Call (January 17)," *Challies* (blog), January 17, 2017, https://www.challies.com/final-call/final-call-january-17/. Also see Theo Hobson, *Reinventing Liberal Christianity* (Grand Rapids, MI: Eerdmans, 2013).
4. Christopher Yuan and Angela Yuan, *Out of the Far Country: A Gay Son's Journey to God; A Broken Mother's Search for Hope* (Colorado Springs: Waterbrook Press, 2011).
5. "Raising Sexually Healthy Children" (seminar, Harvest USA) accessed December 1, 2017, http://harvestusa.org/?s=raising+sexually+healthy+children.
6. Rosaria Butterfield, *The Gospel Comes with a House Key: Practicing Radically Ordinary Hospitality in Our Post-Christian World* (Wheaton, IL: Crossway, 2018).

Chapter 10: Spreading the Word in Diverse Contexts

1. These are real stories, recent stories, with names changed for people's privacy and protection.

General Index

Abraham, 97
Acts, book of, 175n13
Adam and Eve, 24, 47, 62–63, 97; as created in the image of God, 24, 62. *See also* fall, the
Alcorn, Randy, 173n12
Allen, Chad, 57, 58
ambassadors of Christ, 66–69, 84–86; as always being sent, 86–89; disbursement of as an *ephodia* (expense money), 67–68; as relayers of a message, not educators, 86; and the role of *ezer* (helpmeet, suitable helper, or necessary ally) of Christ, 66; and witness of word and deed, 68–69
atheism, 22
Augustine, 82

Billings, J. Todd, 37
Bloesch, Donald, 105
Bonar, Horatius, 42, 46
Brand, Hillary, 50–51

Cameron, James, 94
Chaplin, Adrienne, 50–51
children, evangelism among, 92; the call to evangelize children, 92–93; the charge to evangelize children, 93–95; hearing cries for a savior, 96–100; seizing the moment, 101–3

commitment to the local church, 44–46; and God's commands for the gathered church, 45
Covenant College, 49; theatre webpage of, 50
creation, 23–25
creation mandate. *See* cultural mandate
cultural mandate, 48; and the gospel, 48; and the image of God, 48; merging with the Great Commission, 48

David, 97–98
demons, 26
discipleship, 109–10

Edson, Margaret, 53, 56–57
evangelism, 33–34, 36; and dependence on God, 71–72; as a means to an end, 77; and role models, 14–16; and a turning outward, 13–14, 78; urgency of, 16–18; and visual and verbal witness, 33; and word and deed, 61–62. *See also* children, evangelism among; evangelism, cross-cultural; evangelism, everyday; LGBTQ community, and Christians' practice of daily, ordinary, radical hospitality; university students, evangelism among; workplace, the, evangelism in

Scripture Index

THE GOSPEL **COALITION**

The Gospel Coalition is a fellowship of evangelical churches deeply committed to renewing our faith in the gospel of Christ and to reforming our ministry practices to conform fully to the Scriptures. We have committed ourselves to invigorating churches with new hope and compelling joy based on the promises received by grace alone through faith alone in Christ alone.

We desire to champion the gospel with clarity, compassion, courage, and joy—gladly linking hearts with fellow believers across denominational, ethnic, and class lines. We yearn to work with all who, in addition to embracing our confession and theological vision for ministry, seek the lordship of Christ over the whole of life with unabashed hope in the power of the Holy Spirit to transform individuals, communities, and cultures.

Through its women's initiatives, The Gospel Coalition aims to support the growth of women in faithfully studying and sharing the Scriptures; in actively loving and serving the church; and in spreading the gospel of Jesus Christ in all their callings.

Join the cause and visit TGC.org for fresh resources that will equip you to love God with all your heart, soul, mind, and strength, and to love your neighbor as yourself.

TGC.org

Also Available from the Gospel Coalition

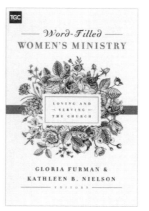

For more information, visit crossway.org.